OUT HERE IN THE OUT THERE

FIRST SERIES: CREATIVE NONFICTION

Philip Heldrich

OUT HERE IN THE OUT THERE

Essays in a Region of Superlatives

MID-LIST PRESS
Minneapolis

Published by Mid-List Press, 4324 12th Avenue South, Minneapolis, MN 55407-3218.
Visit our Web site at www.midlist.org.

Library of Congress Cataloging-in-Publication Data
Heldrich, Philip, 1965–
  Out here in the out there: essays in a region of superlatives/ Philip Heldrich.
    p. cm.
  "First series—creative nonfiction."
  ISBN-13: 978-0-92811-61-8
  ISBN-10: 0-922811-61-X (alk. paper)
  1. Heldrich, Philip, 1965—Homes and haunts—Southwestern States.
2. Southwestern States—Description and travel. 3. Poets, American—20th century—
Biography. 4. Southwestern States—Civilization. I. Title.
  PS3558.E474Z47 2004
  811'.6—dc22

                       2004018875

Printed in the United States of America

Grateful acknowledgment is given to the following journals where these essays first
appeared, sometimes in a slightly altered form: "How I Learned to Shoot Straight" in
Florida Review; "Out Here in the Out There" in *South Dakota Review*; "Curious Abrupt
Questionings: The Lure of Glitz and Glam" in *Weber Studies*; "Parable of the Spiny-
Toothed Gumweed" in *The Heartlands Today*.

    "Out Here in the Out There" was reprinted in the anthology *American Nature
Writing 2001*, ed. John A. Murray (Oregon State University Press, 2001).

    "How I Learned to Shoot Straight" was the winner of the 2001 *Florida Review*
Editor's Award in Nonfiction.

"Albuquerque" by Neil Young © 1973 (renewed) Silver Fiddle Music. All rights
reserved. Used by permission. Warner Brothers Publications U.S. Inc., Miami, FL
33014.

Cover Photo: "Mobil Station 2000" by Don Getsug. Copyright © 2004 by Don Getsug
Cover and text design: Lane Stiles

For Christine and Alexandra

CONTENTS

ACKNOWLEDGMENTS

As with any book, these essays reflect the thoughts, suggestions, and support of many others. I wish to thank Christopher Howell for his belief in the book; Mike Stoffel, my editor, for his keen eye and helpful ideas; and the staff at Mid-List Press, especially Lane Stiles and Marianne Leslie Nora, who helped to bring the book into print.

I also wish to thank R. M., Mr. Tecate Man & Red, The Bear, Jo Jo Love, Hiram Lucke, Larry Schwarm, Scott Richardson, Tim Baker of Tornado Chasers, Peter O'Dwyer "Packer Backer from Down Under," the Emporia D & R Facility, Roberto's, the Girls at Rubi's Frosty Freeze, Lewis at Treasure Island, the Disney Corporation, Peter Donahue, Amy Webb, Kim & Pam, Donna & Jim, Tommy, Bernie & Kelley, Mike, Connie, Gerry, China & Pearl, Christine & Alexandra, as well as the rest of my friends and family, who helped make these essays and journeys possible. And Mom.

The word "topophilia" is a neologism, useful in that it can be defined broadly to include all of the human being's affective ties with the material environment. These differ greatly in intensity, subtlety, and mode of expression. The response to environment may be primarily aesthetic: it may then vary from the fleeting pleasure one gets from a view to the equally fleeting but far more intense sense of beauty that is suddenly revealed. The response may be tactile, a delight in the feel of air, water, earth. More permanent and less easy to express are feelings that one has toward a place because it is home, the locus of memories, and the means of gaining a livelihood. Topophilia is not the strongest of human emotions. When it is compelling we can be sure that the place or environment has become the carrier of emotionally charged events or perceived as symbol.

—Yi-Fu Tuan, *Topophilia: A Study of Environmental Perception, Attitudes, and Values*

Our notions of law and harmony are commonly confined to those instances which we detect; but the harmony which results from a far greater number of seemingly conflicting, but really concurring laws, which we have not detected, is still more wonderful.

—Henry David Thoreau, *Walden*

Signs

OUT HERE IN THE OUT THERE

If one ... looked off at the rough land, the smiling sky, the
curly grass white in the hot sunlight; if one listened to the
rapturous song of the lark, the drumming of the quail, the
burr of the locust against that vast silence, one understood....

—Willa Cather, O Pioneers!

We follow the south wind north, where the county highway
cuts its way through the green Kansas prairie. Even the air
seems green, heavy and moist, so thick it hangs over the rolling
land. Every twenty miles or so, we cross a muddy river snaking
its way slowly east. At this time of the year, the late spring's ver-
dant growth seems as if it will never fade. Before leaving, I told
friends I was headed *out there*, as if *out there* were somewhere to
be properly mapped, a psychic geography of sorts. We—my wife
and I in a truck loaded with camping gear and a cooler of
beer—are actually headed northwest, tracing the contours of
the Central Plains in a desire to discover the immensity and
variety of our prairie, how far it stretches outside its endlessness
in our imaginations. There is something else I'm after: silence,
the very pause and breath of a moment, and what will happen
once I detect its presence, its stealthy spirit. I like to think I will
find it out there, away from the industrial din, traffic, lights, and
perverse smells of our small, Kansas meat-packing town.

There are no other vehicles on the highway. We've been on the road, Kansas back roads, for three hours or more. We need to stretch, so I pull our truck over onto a gravel shoulder before a bridge spanning the Republican River. The river seems static, barely moving. The banks are thick with cottonwood, redbud, and leafy elms, whose roots reach like thick vines from the high-water mark to the dark pools below. From where we stand under the canopy of trees, mosquitoes buzz our ears and small grasshoppers dance about in the tall grass butting the bridge's railing. As the bugs have their way with me, I realize we must now be officially *out there*, since we would never pull over along the roadway to watch a river back home. *Out there* seems to be infectious, a lunacy, a cause to act strangely, or perhaps it's just the humidity and abundance of sun, an electric charge to the air that might grow into an afternoon thunderstorm. Late spring and early summer are tricky seasons on the Plains; things can change and clash quickly.

Out there also seems to be a place of abundant sky and land, land that rolls uninterrupted from river to river. In Kansas and in other parts of the Plains, you need to learn to live with such immensity. There's so much land I've often wondered if we can save urban overcrowding by offering resettlement assistance to folks in big cities, a sort of twenty-first-century Homestead Act. Most people, however, would probably desire to remain in such crowded urban centers, the emptiness of the countryside too overwhelming. Without restaurants, a multiplicity of television stations, the fever of traffic, or the intermittent sound of sirens, city folks would feel lost, swallowed up in this vastness. Most locals wouldn't go for the plan either; they seem to celebrate the emptiness.

I myself have come to appreciate the open land. I spent my childhood playing in the forest preserves of northern Illinois not far from Lake Michigan, woods thick with oak, birch, and maple. But I've been a Kansan long enough now—most of my adult life—to make a peace with treeless stretches of prairie, to know such land needs its distances, its closeness of sky, its sun and rain. Everybody here has to make such a peace. Before settlers came west, tribes such as the Kiowa, Comanche, Wichita, Kaw, Pawnee, and Sioux sang and danced to honor the land, its spirits and gifts. Each tribe in its own particular way understood the land through story and myth, the resplendence of the prairie sun or its wind and corn. This prairie, they knew, was life itself, provider of roots, nuts, herbs, buffalo, deer, turkey, water, and shelter, without which there could be no life. For the Pawnee, such life began with Tirawa, "the Expanse of the Heavens," something akin to first thought, creativity itself, the power behind thunder and lightening. Knowing the land through the imagination makes it possible to understand how a coyote becomes invested with spirit. I've actually seen coyotes make their way over grassy hills, seen their silhouettes against the backdrop of a setting sun, heard their calls bounce between other dogs hidden in the bluestem. In such moments, it's easy to know how story and myth are the only means to truly grasp this animal's tricky presence.

I hear a truck in the distance; although I can't yet see it, I know it's coming, can hear its tires on the pavement. Even before I've had the chance to locate the elusive silence I'm seeking along this river, the moment has passed. My wife, who is careful not to step too far into the shoulder's grasses, walks back to our truck. She knows about chiggers and rattlesnakes, has seen me pull ticks from my legs after walking in a field of tallgrass. A California transplant, she recognizes the dangers of this place, as must have early pioneer women. Like them, she too has sought to make her peace with this land. In the long hours I spent fulfilling the requirements for a graduate degree, she worked at coming to understand the loneliness of prairie life. She knew before I ever did that time here is overwhelming, that it can easily outlast the spirit. To survive, you have to learn to fill the time, fill the space with imagination. We see this land differently. To her it's someplace to survive, while to me it's an enigma waiting to be unraveled, a possibility of sorts in contrast to the woodlands I once knew.

We've made too many stops today to watch rivers or listen to the wind in an open field. When I was a child, my parents always drove the interstates no matter where we went. For a long time, my vision of the country came from brief pit stops at a McDonald's, Pizza Hut, or one of the innumerable Stuckey's. If I had suggested we stop to see a river, my parents might have taken me for counseling when we returned home. To them, the interstate, a marvel of modern engineering, represented the quickest, most efficient way to and from an actual destination. Everything else in between was just something to pass through, to endure. However, in the back seat under a haze of their cigarette smoke, I found a way to keep track of the land by never falling asleep, by taking blurred pictures with my Kodak out of the back window. I took in the countryside until it consumed my imagination, until, upon returning home, I could only think about getting back *out there* to see it all. Throughout my teenage years, I wanted to leave home and the security of its suburban copiousness for the emptiness of the *in between*. My brothers, one in Kansas City and the other in Chicago, think I have "a screw loose" for coming to live where I do in small-town Kansas; to them, I live "in the sticks with the hicks." They rarely come to visit because all they can do is complain about what I don't have, such as cable TV, a Starbucks, a deli of repute, or a good restaurant. They refuse to see what's here, something I'm continually pointing out when they do visit, making the two-hour drive from the city or airport to my town.

Along this Republican River valley, paralleling the Kansas–Nebraska border on which we've been traveling, the prairie changes somewhat from the more defined dips and hills in our part of the state in the east-central Flint Hills region, though it takes a trained eye to see the difference. Up here, the land seems to lean toward the river. To farmers working the fertile bottomlands on both sides of the state line, water is a commodity, enough so Nebraskans have been known to steal it from us Kansans, sometimes in the middle of the night. Red Cloud, the first town we come to in Nebraska, rests some twenty-four miles up the Nebraska side of the long river. When we arrive, the streets largely deserted, we wonder if anybody actually lives in the town.

Red Cloud was named after the Oglala Sioux chief and later peace advocate who fought the U.S. Cavalry in a series of battles begun in 1866 known as Red Cloud's War. Red Cloud's attacks sprang from a series of provocations, including the building of the Union Pacific Railroad, the killing of buffalo upon which the Sioux depended, and the increasing numbers of settlers and miners traveling a new road, the Oregon Trail, to reach gold then recently discovered in Montana. The Great Fort Laramie Treaty of 1868, which Red Cloud signed reluctantly, attempted to stop the fighting, and it did until 1875 with the discovery of gold in the Black Hills, lands ceded to the Sioux in the Treaty that were considered sacred and inviolable to the tribe.

While the Sioux history seems mostly forgotten now, Red Cloud remains a typical prairie town that boomed at the turn of the nineteenth century when pioneers arrived from the East with dreams to cultivate the land free of Indians into something more than it appeared to be. Men came to transform the prairie, subdue it, tame it like their obedient wives. The notion that most folks unprepared for the conditions could tame the prairie was absurd, especially considering the relentless heat of long summers without rain, plagues of grasshoppers and assorted crop-eating insects, the ever-present danger of flash flooding, the clash of winds, lightning, and tornadoes. *Fools!* I'm certain after numerous summers in Kansas that only the truly befuddled would have chosen to remain, and if lucky, prosper.

Hard work alone could not have made a significant impact without good fortune. Everything here eventually turns back into grass.

Red Cloud is most famously remembered not for its Indian namesake but as the hometown of Willa Cather, the place of her childhood exile from the cultured world of the East. A few blocks up from the Republican River, not far from the Red Cloud train depot, she spent the formative years of her life, a time and place she would return to often in her writing. The Willa Cather Pioneer Memorial has preserved the town almost as it must have appeared in Cather's time, in the town's heyday. The limestone bank and brick buildings along Main Street seem timeless, except for a few newer-looking cowboy bars, though they probably had them too in Cather's day. Cather's own house, a small one-story wooden structure with a cramped attic, still stands. In the attic, Cather spent countless hours reading and dreaming of the world beyond the prairie, though she would come to realize that the prairie was itself a significant landscape, a place that's hard to forget because it gets deep into your blood, the way grass roots reach for water. In the summer—today it's a steamy 100-plus degrees—the Cather family slept on cots in the back yard, and in the winter, the attic bedroom with its exposed roof boards and plaster lattice would have been no friendlier to young Cather. For a few moments, at least as many minutes as we can stand the heat, our host allows us to remain in the attic. I try to picture Cather lying on her cot reading the books piled on a nightstand beside her bed. I can almost feel her presence, hear the wind blowing across the prairie, understand the despair of knowing that the town is an island of sorts connected only by the periodic visits of whistling trains. The grasses ripple in the wind as the land rolls away in all directions. The sky is close in Red Cloud, perhaps even closer than in Kansas. For just a second or so, I think I've detected a bit of what I've been searching for, or perhaps what Cather herself noticed here, an elusive and evanescent moment of silence that, when recognized, disappears. In that second or so it takes for my discovery to take place, the floorboards give up a creak, the house rattles a moment in the wind, and our host calls to us to make sure we haven't passed out.

As we walk about the quaint streets of simple wooden homes, I can't stop thinking of Cather. In her books, she created strong women like Alexandra Bergson, women who could, though not always willingly, withstand the rigors of a lonely prairie life filled with hard work. Alexandra, like those Native Americans before her, imagined the possibilities of this prairie place. When she saw her neighbors' crops fail because of insects or drought, she found alternative methods of farming. Alexandra sought not to subdue the land, but to nurture it, plant crops suitable for the climate. With such knowledge, her farm prospered, but at times she could not overcome the loneliness and isolation, much like the homesteading women of the late nineteenth century. The individualism examined and often contested throughout Cather's classic novel seems in stark contrast to the communalism of many Native American Plains cultures. Typically, their myths, though different for each distinct culture, do not reflect ideas of land possession and rugged individualism. Such cultures have no fundamental tradition of a lone man in a battle with nature; instead, they value the self in its relationships to the tribe and the land. Without the tribe, without the cooperation of others and an understanding of the land, the self perishes. Sometimes the ostracized or the sick and aged left the safety of the tribe for the open land. They made such courageous acts with the knowledge that alone as individuals they would eventually pass away.

The ideology of radical individualism is deep within me, something I've learned from a very young age, an appreciation for open spaces and endless vistas, a sense that three is always a crowd. My father, a suburban pioneer, taught me to appreciate the swagger of John Wayne and the films of John Ford, as if the myths they offered could save me from the bane of our homogenized existence in a bedroom community of tract homes and strip malls. Sunday-afternoon television and Saturday matinees with Clint Eastwood provided this western dream like a religion. I wanted to be a cowboy before I ever learned about saddle sores. All my life, I've cultivated self-sufficiency, a do-it-yourself mentality. If I needed others, I found another way to make it work. I don't know the first thing about making preserves, about silage, about what cows eat and how much to water a horse. If I had a bunch of land, I'd know nothing more than how to look at it.

I'm reminded of a student of mine and a class exercise we did to practice our writing skills. The assignment asked for us to examine a "field," to write about what the field might mean. My students took out a blank sheet of paper—its blankness similar to a prairie field itself upon first glance—and began to write, to fill in the empty space. I, too, did the exercise—I always try to do whatever my students do. We wrote for a good ten minutes, then stopped to share our discoveries. We took turns reading our brief paragraphs aloud, marveling at the variety of expression and the use of detail. I was bold enough to share my writing with the class, to set an example of how not to be embarrassed by our exercises. In my writing about a "field," I remember concentrating on the abundance and variety of grasses, the sound of the wind blowing through them, the loneliness of a tree in an empty field—the way I saw such a field that day. Although I don't remember what many of these students wrote about and read aloud after me—though many of them took similar approaches—I do remember the writing of one fellow, a young man at the corner of our rectangular table who grew up in a town of less than five hundred people. To him, a field meant acreage, planting and watering, a sense of hope and failure. In other words, his field was a place of work. He didn't write about the lovely grasses or their golden tops blowing in a gentle breeze. He wrote about tractors and mud, the blood and guts of what a field meant to him and his family, the fact that they lived and perished by the field. Sometimes, I understood, just surviving was an accomplishment. He dropped my class a few weeks later to return to his family farm.

The lessons I learned that day seem clear enough now; there are many ways to see a field. Though our responses were different, we each saw the field in a similar fashion because we held, or hold, a common ideology. To my student, the field represented a place where the hard work of a tenacious individual can, with the grace of a benevolent God, lead to success. To me, the field represented an aestheticized, Edenic space, a beautiful, ahistorical landscape. In other words, we saw the field in that moment from the two sides of the very paradox that makes up the American mythology of the West: the awesome, inspiring, virgin land represents potential capital, though once worked, or spoiled by human hands, its beauty, its purity and innocence, its place outside history ceases to exist.

As the late afternoon takes shape with the sky's golden hue the color of ripening wheat, we leave Red Cloud, passing one aged farmhouse after another along the county highway. Such structures, painted white like beacons or islands of refuge across an inland sea, are generally two, sometimes three, stories. By no means do these homes desire to be audacious, preferring to remain as modest as their stolid owners. They are usually set back about a quarter mile from the highway and are often a mile or more away from their closest neighbor. There is generally a hedgerow of osage to act as a windbreak along the windiest side of the home; sometimes there's a barn, or the remains of a barn, and usually an old silo, its top blown off decades ago. These homes, with their utilitarian appearance, seem metaphors for the families who dwell within them. They are visual symbols of the radical individual, similes of loneliness, like the long laundry lines blowing in an incessant wind. All day we have passed by such homes, some abandoned and a number in considerable decay, just as with the small Midwestern family farm, a victim of corporate farms and American big business. These homes seem more like ruins, American ruins of a previous century, a former day's dream. Across the Plains, such homes are returning, literally, to the earth from which they came. Some communities like Red Cloud fight against the encroaching future by clinging to their proud past, to the dream it once represented, an American myth of sorts.

Most Americans live now in suburbs and in large cities. In such buffer zones of activity and noise, beltways of safety against the land beyond, people need cell phones and tires that won't deflate for sixty miles after puncture. They seem to have an implicit fear of the land, an anxiety of separation, of being too far from the mall, the Quick Mart, the movie store. My brothers are such people. They think I've flipped out, regressed somehow from the rightful way to suburban bliss. It's amazing they haven't tried to kidnap me for an intervention. I think I'm one of the few who still dare to drive open spaces on county roads with little more than a full tank of gas, a ham sandwich, and a thermos of coffee.

The fears of suburbanites are not to be taken lightly. In fact, I've come face to face with the very people they fear, and fear for good reason. One time, on a lonely stretch of highway outside Wellington, Kansas, my then-ten-year-old Ford broke down and I needed a tow. After hiking to the phone to call for help on an evening when the temperature pressed 100, a local tower came to pick me up. A city dweller's worst nightmare, the obese man had rotten and missing teeth, a T-shirt covered in engine grease, dirty fingernails, and hadn't shaved for days. His arms and hands, one of which I had to shake when he arrived, were thick with fat. His balding head and neck sweated profusely, reddened from sunburn. His appearance alone would have scared most folks away, but when he assured me—by all means truly seeking to be comforting—that I would be safe in his town for the night because there "were no niggers," I wished

I'd had that cell phone. With this fellow, you could never be sure if bedsheets were for sleeping or wearing. Racism in our culture, in a nation espousing the sanctity of the individual over community, runs deep as the Midwest's muddy rivers, rivers separating White from Black, from Red, from Brown. Cities are really no different with their concentric zones of urban poverty, their 'hoods and housing projects; perhaps people just aren't so blunt in cities, preferring to say polite things like "stay away from the 'bad' side of town," "bad" a commonly understood signifier for nonwhite. In Wellington, I had realized my brothers' worst fears about the dangerous, ignorant country-side. I'm reminded of a comment Amiri Baraka once jokingly told me over dinner when he came to Emporia a few years back for a Black History Month reading. While eating a Louisiana gumbo a colleague of mine in Education made from his mother's recipe, Baraka said that long ago Blacks in the South left rural America for cities up north because it was no longer safe out in the country. At the time, his facetiousness masked the truth of his statement to most of those in the room, but because of my experience in Wellington, I knew exactly what he meant. Kenneth Lincoln in his memoir *Men Down West* has described similar poor race relations in the town of Alliance, Nebraska, where Sioux families live separated from the town's white population. Many folks passing through see the Plains and its people as all the same, but the Plains do not have a homogeneous population, and more so now with rapidly growing immigration from Mexico and Central America for work in the slaughter-houses of western Kansas and the Oklahoma Panhandle. In fact, the people are more heterogeneous, like the prairie itself, a concert of angles and inclines, dips and hills, grasses and flow-ers. Like glancing at an Impressionist painting, these travelers haven't looked long enough to see the varied lights and ter-rains, the fine shadowing, how the intricate dots of various paints render an entire picture.

Well beyond Red Cloud in the middle of the Nebraska sand hills, a region in the center of the state that most people would consider as *out there* as possible, we make camp. It's a peaceful, contoured prairie landscape, carved by cutting winds and erosive rain. The grass is shorter here than to the south, the soil a sandy loam the color of oatmeal. Things pass through here, too, rivers and automobiles, cold fronts and warm fronts, lots of coal trains from Wyoming. It's a moist night, the dew thick on the grass. Since it's only late spring, the mosquitoes have not yet reached their peak numbers, but frogs on a small pond are singing their hearts out. It's a lovesickness that hangs in the air like the evening mist. We're nearly the only ones at the Victoria Springs state campground five miles from the county highway and not far down the road from the oxymoronic Nebraska National Forest. The ranger and his family live in a cabin near the entrance. In our truck's headlights, we pitch our small tent and set up our Coleman stove to cook a quick dinner of hot dogs and beans, camping food. Back home, I hardly touch the stuff, but when camping, hot dogs and beans is the meal of choice, easy to prepare, easy to clean up, and hearty. We're good at cooking in the dark. We've done it in camp-grounds across America, always arriving well past the dinner hour after a full day on the road.

We generally try to pick campgrounds off the beaten path, such as this one five miles past the last road sign to nowhere. It's hard to believe they even have a campground out here, but the ranger assures me it's very busy during hunting season. I try to picture men in camouflage, with shotguns and Miller beer, as they lean against their pickups, a bloody deer in the back. It's not a comforting picture, so I make a note to avoid this place in November. Otherwise, it's lovely and well kept here. I've been a camping devotee since my early years as a Boy Scout; and, while pursuing my education—years I've come to equate with a monastic vow of poverty—tent camping became the only way my wife and I could afford to vacation. In many ways I'm glad we didn't have the money; I can think of few better ways two people can share time together. When you camp, sharing and cooperation are essential. Perhaps all adolescents should be required to camp for a week or more to learn about community and sharing, about working together and accepting one another. In the close quarters of a tent or campground, it's hard to do much else.

While holidays are among the few times people can get away from the drudgery of their jobs to commune with the outdoors, we stay home to avoid the crowds. Campgrounds do have their limitations. I've been to places where kids run in packs like coyotes, where inside an RV, campers watch television and movies. I remember one campground in New Mexico where a fellow was running a gas-powered electric generator. The smoke and the noise blew uninterrupted into our tent site. When I could stand it no longer, I went to confront the man in his metal can where he watched TV with his children. I hated to spoil such a family moment, but I had to remind him that there were other people in the campground who came to listen to the wind blowing through the pines and to see the stars. He looked at me as if I had lost my mind, then begrudgingly turned off his machine. "I'm doing this as a favor to you," he told me. I need not say more.

Sometimes you can't avoid such places or such people; the great outdoors can seem to be a shrinking place. I like to believe that we all come to such places in search of the same things, to enjoy the natural world, to find a moment of peace and quiet, to avoid as many people as we can. However, my wife has told me that some families with children like to come to be with other families with children. I remind her that that's why they built suburbs, but she feels I'm a bit eccentric in my opinions at times. I used to believe my love of the outdoors was a natural thing, that the human condition desired it, but I know I'm wrong. In fact, I have friends who think camping is anything but natural; to them it's a perversity of sorts, sleeping on the ground, eating beans on a tin plate, slathering on bug juice—I don't bother to tell them about going to the bathroom. However, I believe the outdoors can heal. Perhaps it's just another American ideology I can trace to my love of the Concord Transcendentalists, even to Jonathan Edwards when not preaching Hell's fire. I've read too much Emerson and Thoreau, too much Whitman, too much Edward Abbey. I believe so much in nature I've come to see it as truth. William Stafford once said, "The world can save you; it can make you strong." I believe him. All you have to do is walk into it, accept its presence. The prairie works this way too, brings you closer to the very pulse of the universe.

Tonight there is not a cloud in the sky. The air from the north has a slight chill to it, as if you can feel the lingering spirit of winter. On the prairie on such a night, there are too many stars to count, too many worlds to know, too much black space to feel comfortable in. I try to find a few recognizable points of light: the Big Dipper, Orion's Belt, the North Star. Without such stellar markers, I'm lost, like Coronado in western Kansas; he eventually had to use a sextant to navigate the prairie after becoming disoriented. For a moment, I think the prairie has sighed, held its breath for just a second. In the brevity of this moment, I know I've found the silence I've sought. It lasts only as long as it takes me to recognize it. It happens that fast, like a breath, then vanishes. In the distance, a coyote howls and another responds, like bats sending sonar across the sand hills. These are wayward hearts desperately needing one another, *out there* crying to fill the encompassing void. Out here in the *out there* is comforting; it's what I'll take with me when we leave. But in this moment, I recognize something more true than the silence I've sought—the prairie's modus operandi is not silence but symphony, each voice, each wisp of wind a subtle reminder that this land is alive. There's an inherent vibrancy, the verve of the charged spirit. Every frog and prairie wolf, every cricket and mosquito, every dragonfly and June bug sings with its own timbre in a chorus that rises and falls, stutters and clamors, but rarely ceases to resonate, except perhaps for a brief breath between notes. If I listen hard enough, I can hear a faint drumbeat in these hills, a heartbeat of sorts, a spectacular song and dance.

HOW I LEARNED TO SHOOT STRAIGHT

*I think George Washington owned guns. I've never seen
any contradiction with that … I believe I have every right
to have guns. I just bought another huge weapon. A lot of
people shouldn't own guns. I should. I have a safety
record. Guns are a lot of fun out here.*

—Hunter S. Thompson

*After a shooting spree, they always wanna take the guns
away from the people who* didn't *do it. I sure as hell
wouldn't want to live in a society where the only people
allowed guns are the police and the military.*

—William S. Burroughs, "The War Universe"

Aim

About an hour from Denver not far from Loveland Pass and the
high-dollar homes of Aspen, I'm in a high country meadow
shooting guns at daybreak with my good buddy Reb. The clatter we're making this crisp Sunday in May must have the deer
checking their calendars; the crows, too, are agitated, cawing at
us to stop as they scatter from pine to pine. Perhaps we should
have brought earplugs, though this isn't a sport for sissies. Fifty

yards ahead of us are a number of sizeable boulders with hay bales stacked up in front of them in a chest-high row. Pinned to the bales are typical range targets with their tiny red sweet spots. Across the tops of these bales are a line of Coors beer cans, some freshly emptied, our breakfast, others riddled with holes like a cheese grater. Spread across a picnic blanket are Reb's guns from a large collection left to him by his rich uncle, or so the story goes. There's a slew of them, expensive handguns, rifles, and automatics with recognizable names: Glock, Ruger, Colt, Beretta, Benelli, Smith & Wesson, Browning, Winchester, Uzi, and Styr.

"Hold your hand steady," Reb shouts, a Colt .45 "Peacemaker" heavy in my hand. "Don't think too hard about it. Just shoot," he says. Reb knows; he always hits his targets.

Like Wyatt Earp on the streets of Dodge, I unload, my wrist snapping from the kickback. "Try two hands," Reb yells. "You're no Clint Eastwood." Hitting bales is much easier than targets, though with every shot I feel more and more charged up, a feeling of exhilaration rising from my loins to my grip. The next shot I take with the gun slung low at my hip, the way cowboys look in westerns. A few shots later, I'm addicted like Reb, who fires shot after shot with his Beretta until he shreds his target, the echo of our fire ringing in the distance, perhaps all the way to Aspen.

The land we're turning into Swiss cheese belongs to one of Reb's clients in his computer security business. According to Reb, the landowner is a well-off Denver businessman who also has an affection for guns. Both Reb and his client belong to the Libertarian Party, where they met. Another buddy of mine in Vegas has also recently joined the party; he e-mails me a barrage of propaganda to entice me to join. For months now, Reb too has been sending me pamphlets about the party, though I remain steadfastly an independent. For Reb, the Libertarians seemed to have picked up his spirit, given him a cause. He needs such causes to keep him preoccupied, plagued all his life by periodic bouts of depression.

Since Reb has become a Libertarian—not to be confused with libertine, I tell him—he says stuff like how he can drive as fast as he wants on the interstate since tickets don't matter, how the federal government has no jurisdiction to regulate highways owned by the citizens, who pay, he says, illegal taxes (I'm writing this the way he actually says it, all from a man who drives an '81 Honda Civic that crawls up mountainsides at a slug's pace). He vows, if cited for speeding, which I can't imagine, that he'll be his own lawyer, too. He says all this with enough confidence that I actually begin to believe him. I can't help thinking how his twisted logic about the government, true or not, sounds strangely like that of terrorists Tim McVeigh, Terry Nichols, and Ted Kaczinski. In Reb's defense, I must say that he is one of the kindest and most peaceable people I know. I can't imagine him using his vast collection of legal and illegally altered weapons for injurious purposes, including hunting—at least that's what I tell myself as I fire away, still hoping I'll hit a target.

"Try this for better luck," Reb says, tossing me his Browning .22. I'm familiar with the .22, shot one years ago at Boy Scout camp at a similar, though more supervised, shooting range. Back then, I even believed I could actually hit a target, especially after days of practice and guidance by the BSA sharpshooter, a German-born man with short blond hair, a square head and prominent jaw, who spoke with an accent similar to Arnold Schwarzenegger's in *Terminator* or Colonel Klink's in *Hogan's Heroes*. "Das gut," he would tell me, "yur gettink bettor." The range was the only thing at camp that cost money, though with an attorney father who probably preferred to have me away for the summer, I had an endless supply of funding.

"How much of this land belongs to your client?" I ask, looking at the NO TRESPASSING signs nailed to various pines dotting the sides of the range.

"About as far as you can see in any direction," Reb returns. "He calls this place his wildlife preserve, has a strict no kill policy. Can't shoot the hares, can't shoot the bears. He comes up in deer season to guard the animals. You might say he's got a soft side for Bambi." Like his client, Reb, too, is as much of a contradiction as anybody I know.

We continue shooting, unable to do much talking over the noise. It's not like we often make a lot of chatter—we're men, for God's sake. We tell tales, real or imagined, not confessing our feelings as one might to his parish priest or to his ex-wife in divorce court. For example, Reb never tells me he's depressed about his family or his work, his future or his income; though when he drops off my radar for a couple of months or sounds like he has the flu when I call, I know something is up. It's what goes unsaid between men that matters the most.

"Try this," Reb shouts, giving me an Uzi. The assault weapon is lighter than I remember, though years ago, after the assault weapons ban of '86, I did briefly hold an Uzi in my hands, the weapon of choice for a cocaine-dealing neighbor of mine in Del Mar, California, "Where the Surf Meets the Turf" and there are plenty of people who can afford cocaine habits. The neighbor, despite the way he financed his living, made a good drinking buddy; the booze and extras were always at his expense. After a few rounds of tequila or some Jack, he enjoyed bragging not only about his line of work—no pun intended—but his guns, his "Betty" (steady girlfriend), his "ladies" (sex partners), and his Porsche Carrera. As long as he was providing my liquor, he could tell me anything he wanted, like how the Swedish ambassador's prodigal son was a steady customer of his—a stunning and intriguing story I only disclose, if true, at the risk of an international incident. My neighbor also bragged that he once sat next to Bob Hope at the Del Mar Racetrack, the same place that holds gun shows throughout the winter when the track facilities, the Del Mar Fairgrounds, are used for little more than environmentally detrimental grand prix racing or prom nights.

I once went to one of these gun shows with my roommate at the time, a fellow who also had an affection for weapons and heavy drinking. It was my virgin gun-show experience. I expected little but men with tattoos in Harley Davidson T-shirts trading weapons with friends. My roommate was a motor-bike enthusiast himself, preferring a cheaper, high-strung Japanese cock rocket to the slow rumble of an expensive Milwaukee-made Hawg. However, the show seemed populated more by your average white neighbors than any admirers of the Hell's Angels. At the show, I felt like the ultimate outsider among insiders who conversed about guns in terms too technical for me to ever confidently replicate—bullet and barrel sizes, models and millimeters, as if they were comparing their dicks in a junior high locker room.

The fairground's exhibition hall is a large place, warehouse large, able to accommodate entire indoor gardens each June during the annual Del Mar Fair. This same room also houses a yearly bridal show with hundreds of engaged and worried brides-to-be and their mothers. In other words, the room is big, so big I couldn't even see from one end to the other. Now picture this, display table after display table filled with guns, probably on average ten guns per person, which means some had five and others fifty. What I saw was an arsenal able to defend Nepal from the Chinese, not to mention able to protect suburbia from urban threats such as bus routes from downtown that terminate at the neighborhood mall. The show's awesome display of power, of revolutions and civil wars, would give Rambo pause, and all in the wealthy seaside village of Del Mar.

Seeing the copious weaponry, new and old, antique and high tech, I was reminded of an experience years ago with Reb in a Cook County, Illinois, forest preserve just outside Wheeling, not far from our hometown. When legislators of Cook County created preserves with the Forest Preserve Act of 1905, which by the fall of 1916 would begin the purchase of property to protect the vanishing Great Lakes woodlands, nobody could have predicted how these preserves would also provide cover for drug and weapons dealers, often the same person serving both roles. Some preserves became famous less for the trees than for the readily available cheap dope—not to mention, had you had the money or desire, the additional lure of cocaine, amphetamines, and LSD. For reasons unclear to me to this day, the Cook County authorities rarely visited such makeshift Narco Marts, even though, I would assume, people must have known about the illegal activities.

Curious about what we had heard of a particular preserve and wanting to see it for ourselves, Reb and I drove there after school one afternoon in my '71 Ford Maverick, a car so rusty that on snowy days road sleet blew up into the cab through the floorboards. I should mention, in defense of the preserve, that it was a popular place to fish for catfish. With our fishing poles and a can of worms in the back seat, Reb and I idled down the preserve's driveway of dealers, everybody shouting out something for sale. Next to where we decided to cast out our lines, we came across a fellow selling not only cheap bags of pot but police revolvers for seventy-five dollars out of his truck filled up to the brim with weapons. It's hard to say how my life might have turned out if I had bought a revolver or had had the desire to knock off 7-Elevens, savings and loans, or people who simply got in my way—and all if I could have shot straight.

That day at the preserve, just as on that afternoon at the Del Mar gun show, I didn't buy a weapon. However, if I were a criminal or a paranoid suburbanite, I would have found the gun show to be the best place possible for an anonymous weapons purchase. It seems obvious to me now how Tim McVeigh could have financed the Oklahoma City bombing with money from the sale of stolen weapons at gun shows, where there are hundreds of folks with a weapons lust similar to my enthusiasm for French wine.

Safety

Things I shot at with my older brother's Daisy CO2-enhanced pistol (the one my mother never knew about and, if she had, would have promptly confiscated for disposal): Lots of birds (*though I don't remember hitting any*), lots of squirrels (*again, never actually hit any*), the windows of the grammar school across the street, stop signs, passing trains, friends, more passing trains, bottles, cans, and other kids on bikes riding by our house when my mother was out grocery shopping or having her hair done at Charlotte's.

Close encounters where a firearm almost discharged in my presence, not including hunting or recreational shooting: My grandmother with a snub-nose revolver who, on a drunken binge, showed up at our back door to shoot my father, whom she detested for reasons too numerous to list here; a bank holdup outside Walgreen's in Northbrook, Illinois, where I was told by police to duck for protection behind my rusty Ford Maverick with the holey floorboards.

Actual discharges: My neighbor who shot raccoons out of his tree because they were, in his words, "a nuisance"; a high school acquaintance who unloaded his father's 12-gauge in their small, uncarpeted, concrete basement to demonstrate, in his words, "the spray."

Gun shops where I reside in Emporia, Kansas, pop. 25,000—closest major city, Topeka, one hour north; closest town, Olpe, pop. 431, 11 miles south; Dodge City, 239 miles west; Washington, D.C., 1529 miles east: Emporia Gun & Pawn, City Pawn, Wal-Mart, the Gun Den, and John's Gun Shop in Olpe (Lock, Stock & Bible, I discovered, is only a Christian bookstore).

National Rifle Association Field Rep: Tel. 620-3**-6643. (Due to liability issues, I am unable to publish the number. However, a good gumshoe could easily track it down.)

Bumper stickers around town: "I'm Out of Estrogen and I Have a Gun!" (on three cars in my campus parking lot), "My Wife, My Car, But Not My Gun" (on Ford Bronco outside Liquor Locker), "Protected by Smith & Wesson" (on my divorced neighbor's leased Chevy pickup), "Glock Pistols" (on my divorced neighbor's leased Chevy pickup), "Piss on Clinton" (on my divorced neighbor's leased Chevy pickup).

Brief thought: Emporia is either a very paranoid town, a very safe town, or a very dangerous town, all depending on whether or not the IBP slaughterhouse, the Dolly Madison bakery, or the Modine plant will lay off workers and on how much booze such workers drink after their shifts at places like Bruff's Tavern (with its infamous bullet in the wall leftover from a murder). So far, I think I've been very lucky here, not counting the night the police apprehended a renegade teen in bloody fisticuffs outside the front door of my apartment where the teen had run for cover; I also don't hold it against the police or the apartment manager that I had to clean up the boy's blood myself from my door and hallway walls.

Discharge

Across the Great Plains and the West, gun enthusiasm is ubiquitous, a part of the culture not unlike blue jeans, rodeos, and burritos. In Emporia, cowboys and wannabe-cowboys carry guns on racks in their pickups, even when deer are not in season, just in case, I assume, they come across a road sign that is not yet riddled with shotgun spray. My students openly confess to such road sign maiming, mostly occurring from a speeding pickup— "What else is there to do around here?" they complain. To practice sign shooting, there is a gun club's target range south of Emporia's Cottonwood River. On most days, the rolling Flint Hills, with some of the last tallgrass prairie in America, is a quiet, serene place where cattle can run roughshod over a fragile prairie ecosystem, but on Saturdays, the Dry Creek range, busier than a mall in Kansas City, has enough action to worry even the largest field bulls.

A colleague of mine recently moved into an old farmhouse a few fields over from the gun range. When I first visited her on a weeknight as the sun set over the lush green hills to the west, I thought she had moved into a country paradise, a place where it's possible to drink Lynchburg Lemonade on the porch without hearing the town's ever-present industrial din; I thought such until I had the pleasure of visiting on a Saturday, when the incessant pop of bullets from the gun club seemed adequate competition for a hailstorm.

Sure, it's easy to criticize, satirize, and moralize when it comes to guns. And I must confess, as a gun owner myself, I'm a part of the problem. In fact, I like to shoot, even though I can't hit a thing except large road signs or an occasional pheasant. When an Ivy League friend of mine once visited from Maine, I suggested to him we go shoot skeet. "It's a lot of fun," I said, convincing him to slum with the gun-toting locals; he had a great time and hit much more than I could. And when I visit my brother-in-law in Bullhead, Arizona, he always extends an invitation to put holes in the cacti. Perhaps I receive so many invitations for gunplay because I'm a good shooting buddy, someone with worse aim. As a boy I had the fantasy of being an Olympic biathlete; I could cross-country ski, but I sure couldn't shoot straight.

Such a fascination with guns also runs in my family. It didn't take long for my aunt and uncle to become gun nuts when they moved, during a midlife crisis, from New Jersey to Keystone, Colorado. When I visited them with my new bride on our honeymoon, they insisted on taking us to their favorite local gun shop. "We're thinking of making a purchase," they confessed, "when we get the money." At the time they were renting a cramped one-bedroom condo and leasing a Ford Explorer, living from paycheck to paycheck.

The gun shop we visited was typical: an arsenal of rifles and shotguns racked on a wall behind glass cases displaying hand-guns of all shapes and sizes. The clerk himself, a bearded man with a sizeable belly, seemed knowledgeable enough for a career in the ATF, if only he could pass their physical, and if forearms covered in blue tattoos weren't a problem. My uncle preferred an older, military-issue rifle, which he said reminded him of his gun from Nam. My aunt, with her periodic vocalized "pow-pows," liked the purse-sized Saturday night specials—the "pea-shooters," she called them. That night, the clerk must have showed them each ten to twelve different models, while my wife nudged me about how late it seemed to be getting. A sub-urban Los Angelina who has never shot a gun, she had yet to appreciate the freedoms expressed by, the symbolism of, the technological achievements to be found in a good old American gun shop. That night was my wife's first and last gun shop experience. We have yet to visit the aunt and uncle again.

Backfire

Reb too had an uncle fascinated with weapons. The guns with us on the mountain today comprise only a part of Reb's vast arsenal mailed to him from Miami after his uncle passed away. For decades I'd heard stories about this uncle, but secretly I believed the man to be a figment of Reb's vast imagination. As the story goes, the rich uncle, or more accurately, great-uncle, lived on a large estate off the Intracoastal waterway; he had an Olympic-size swimming pool, palm trees and tropical flowers, a well-landscaped lawn, a boat, a maid, and, of course, plenty of guns. The uncle, more like somebody from *Lifestyles of the Rich and Famous*, seemed too unreal to be Reb's uncle.

Sure, Reb would occasionally claim to go visit the uncle, though when he returned without a tan, I would become sus-picious, wondering if maybe he had spent his vacation with less glamorous relatives in the more humble state of Indiana. I even developed a theory that Reb's tall tales about this uncle grew from his childhood in a divided family, with a father who left before Reb turned five and a mother given to bouts of heavy drinking. Perhaps it was really Reb's Irish blood that had a hand in his pale skin and his stories—he once appeared on the *Phil Donahue Show* to swear off teen drinking before millions of MADD mothers across America, then joined me for a few beers that evening. Reb had good reasons for avoiding the sun; his fair skin quickly turned a beet red. Such a skin condition would even explain his stories of swimming at night in his uncle's pool with a teenage girl from the estate next door. While I can believe his nocturnal belly flops, I remain unconvinced about the girl, indeed lovely in his fictions and a topic of our conversations for many years. (Would such a girl really fall for an acne-faced teenager who sent away in the mail for books like *How to Pick Up Women* with the special bonus copy of *101 Best Pickup Lines?*)

Nevertheless, while Reb's stories continued over the years, I always figured there would come a day when, secure with himself and his genius, he would feel ready to leave behind such tales. When he called a few weeks ago to tell me the uncle had passed on, I was certain that day had come. "I'm sorry," I told him. "You must feel terrible."

"I'm all right," he continued. "He'd been sick for a long time. I've been feeling pretty down. I guess I should feel better. He did leave me some dough and his entire gun collection."

"You're a lucky man," I told him. "You'll feel better. Give it time."

"Maybe you could drive out. We could do some shooting. Can you believe it's already been five months since you were out here last?"

"I'll see what I can do," I told him, worried that he might be falling into another depression. "The semester will be over by the end of the week."

After a marathon Friday-night grading session, I hopped into my car early the next morning for the eight-hour drive to Denver. As I drove through the lonely flatlands of western Kansas, covered with the green hope of spring wheat, I couldn't help but think how depression had been a recurring problem for most of Reb's life. Perhaps it was a side effect of having electrocuted himself by accident when seeking to modify a high-voltage generator for one of his home electricity experiments; or perhaps it was just in his blood, the way birds navigate when migrating. Then again, maybe it was just his genius, his difference from 99.9 percent of the population. It's hard to describe just what makes a genius until you have met one; however, I feel most certain it has to do with a person's uncommon vision, that there must be an accompanying sense of loneliness in being a lone voice on society's margins.

If you met Reb, you would most likely think he was simply "strange." Maybe it would be his funny name or how he talks in a flurry of words. Or maybe it would be his uncommon vision, his eyes able to focus in different directions at once (perhaps that's what gives him good aim). To him, a glass isn't half empty or half full, it's how you can see when looking through the water. During his teen years, Reb periodically jumped off his roof, not to kill himself, he said, but to know what went through his mind during the fall. It's not surprising to me that even without the privileges of college he became a successful inventor. I knew it was his future career in the eighth grade when he invented a heat lamp to keep his mother's eggs from going cold while he cooked his own.

With his deceased uncle's money and guns, Reb's life as an inventor could finally take a fortuitous turn. As any inventor knows—and I once dated the daughter of the man who invented the electric garage-door opener, a man who sold his patent during desperate financial straits—it can seem an excruciatingly long time for an idea to become a marketable or successful product. After pioneering a digital decoder and scrambler, Reb was now working on an innovation to the sticky-note by adding a small, red, blinking LED that would draw attention to messages of priority. "They'll be using them in every kitchen and office in America," he had told me over the phone during one of our weekly conversations. "I have a manufacturer in Taiwan now working on the prototype." Reb had come a long way as an inventor; it wasn't until the minor successes of his scrambler that he could come to count on a source of income. His future in inventing seemed an apt alternative to employment as a rail-line coolie, taxi driver, or dishwasher, jobs Reb once held when living out of the back of an old Buick. While I never had the chance to meet Thomas Edison, though I have visited his winter laboratory in Florida, I've always considered Reb to be an Edison of sorts. Like Edison, Reb never slept much.

Sport

While Reb loads the Uzi, I walk across the field to place back onto the wall of hay bales the fallen, pocked cans of Coors beer. As I set up the cans, I can't help but think how lucky Reb and I have been, how up here in the Rockies seems like a million miles from our roots in Illinois, from the oak tree in Riverwoods where Reb crashed his mother's Chevy for the insurance, then walked back home fifteen miles. We finally live in the Wild West, once only a place of our imaginations, of skiing, gun fights, and Coors beer. I turn for a moment to take a look at Reb busy with his guns. He looks good, a bit red in the face from the sun and beer, but happy nonetheless. He doesn't seem too depressed, though that really wouldn't be something we'd talk about, not directly anyway. There might be signs, but you have to look for them, know how to gather them into a story. If his elation masks depression, then maybe I'm onto something.

After setting up the cans and adding a freshly finished one, I walk back to Reb who hands me the reloaded Uzi ready for action. "It's easy to shoot," he says, "just squeeze the trigger and point. With hummers like these," he tells me, "it doesn't matter how your aim is." Like Reb, I plant my feet in the mud, sure of nothing but that if I point the short barrel at the hay bales, I'll hit something—perhaps that's what William Burroughs himself thought just before he missed the glass on his wife's head and instead shot her through the forehead. When Reb commences firing, I squeeze my trigger, too. For a few moments, there's a jackhammer clatter and echo so forceful it rattles my brain, but cans are effortlessly popping off the wall in a spray of hay. In our rain of bullets, I feel a powerful surge. Reb too has a satisfying grin across his face, happier than I've seen him in months. We're soaring, sharing a moment both of our uncles would have appreciated. Neither of us stops shooting until we've spent our cartridges, my ears ringing like sirens. Then there's a momentary silence before we begin reloading, a calm between us so loud only the crows' distant warnings finally shatter it.

In memoriam, R.M.,
killed three months later cleaning a loaded weapon

PARABLE OF THE SPINY-TOOTHED GUMWEED

What we lack most keenly is a sense of beauty and the love of it.... The Kansas prairies are as mysterious and moody as the sea in their loveliness, yet we graze them and plow them and mark them with roads and do not see them.

—William Allen White, "Kansas: A Puritan Survival"

I must begin with a confession: I pick flowers. Perhaps my obsession began as a child seeking to please my mother with a fresh bunch of pilfered cuttings from a neighbor's garden. I was attracted to the names, even the sounds as they rolled off my tongue—foxglove, blue rocket larkspur, forget-me-not, phlox, Swan River daisy, spider flower. The colors too had appeal: indigo, periwinkle, lavender. To me a snapdragon hybrid demonstrated it was possible to combine colors like the eyes of my family—blue-green, greenish-blue, chestnut brown, red after drinking. Or maybe I learned that only by picking the flower is it possible to experience the flower by holding it up to the nose, feeling the cilia against the cheek, grinding a petal between the fingers, or blowing the seeds into the wind. I might pick the flat, oval leaves off a milkweed just to see the cream bubble up like blood in a pricked fingertip. I've even been tempted into sampling what I pick; the acrid petals of spring lilac taste nothing as lovely as their smell.

If supplies are ample, I've been known to make impromptu pullovers onto a roadside shoulder to have a go at the local varieties. I like to head out picking after a spring or summer shower, when the air is freshest, the pollen at its lowest, the colors washed clean by the rain. Sure, my sneakers or sandals might get wet and muddy, but damp feet are nothing compared to the evanescent and earthly pleasure of a freshly picked bouquet of prairie wildflowers. I was once told that flowers in a home bring good luck and prosperity. In times when my only luck is bad, I head to the fields. Rarely do I go to a florist; however, I have been known, when desperate, to brave an ice storm in January for an iris or lily out of season, as if I can take home a hint of the Caribbean or help out the sagging economy of a Central American nation. At our summer farmers' market, I will occasionally buy cultivated flowers grown by a septuagenarian in our town's garden club. I do this more out of support for the market than for the flowers, which often have a distinct appearance of perfection uncommon in wild varieties, of having been grown with fertilizers, pesticides, and herbicides. Such blooms appear as proper as girls in white dresses at junior high dances, stiff as their boyfriends in clip-on ties.

If the roads permit, the greatest wildflower yields can be found along infrequently traveled back roads. I drive them in my thirteen-year-old Ford Escort, the struts no better than an old runner's knees, tires spitting gravel against what remains of my rusted muffler. I like to tell myself that anything from the roadbed to a fence line is open season, free for the picking, though I have reached through barbed wire to grab a bunch of near-blooming, red and yellow heads of Oklahoma blanket flower (if you've never seen the sunset in Oklahoma in the middle of the summer, you can see it in a stand of blanket flower). In the Flint Hills of Kansas, not far from home, the roadbeds are nicely firm, the rolling fields almost endless, the way they've been for thousands of years. Each season from mid-March to early April, the ranchers around here burn these fields, which creates in the months following near-perfect conditions for summer flowers, as if fire itself warms the good earth in its passing, the ashes fertilizing new growth.

I have another confession to make: I pick flowers outside our local dump and recycling facility, the D & R. The buildings stand on the north side of the street across from the waste pools of the IBP meat-processing plant in the southwest corner of Emporia, Kansas. If the south wind blows over the cesspools, I would not recommend picking flowers or recycling anything at the D & R facility. If Hades had a stench, it was modeled on that of the IBP slaughterhouse, something similar to rotten dog food and sewage mixed with the stink of rotting corpses, and worse on a hot day. Tall chain-link fences topped with three rows of razor-sharp wire and NO TRESPASSING signs posted every three yards guard the lagoons that deter even me from approaching. In the distance there is a platformlike structure resembling a guard tower, and there's no telling what kinds of chemicals seep from a cylindrical holding tank at the lagoon's edge. I can only imagine what it takes to "clean" the wastewater before it's sent off in a pipe to our local river or drained onto some of the last tallgrass prairie in America, where I often travel for flowers.

When I go on my trips to this part of town, which I've fondly named the Bowels of Emporia, I also bring what I need to recycle: newspaper and tin cans, aluminum and glass of assorted colors, plastic and cardboard, and an occasional phone book. Our phone directory is only about a quarter of an inch thick, encompassing twenty-seven towns from Admire to Westphalia, half of those listings Yellow Pages, from "Abortion Alternatives" (one listing, open MWF 11:00–4:00) to "Youth Organizations & Centers," (three listings, if you count twice the two entries for the same Girl Scout troop). At the D & R, they pile recycled phone books like garden stones. They're a valuable commodity here with an average of two sheets of coupons for pizza, oil changes, and haircuts at the back of every book. My favorite coupon is for the Caribbean Sun Tanning

Salon, "good August–December," just when Kansans most need a tan before the busy holiday season. In small-town America, it pays to have a nice tan, especially if you're shooting pool under the dim lights at Bruff's Tavern or sucking down a longneck with ranch hands at the Lariat. In a town of some thirty thousand (I think the numbers, which do not include our migrant workforce, are inflated to attract industry), a good tan and a short skirt can open up opportunities, especially at the Flying-J truck stop or the Cabaret U.S.A. stripper bar, which advertises free rides for truckers to and from our local service stations.

"Pass with Care"

Eccentricity is not uncommon to our town. My stand-up line that's not so funny to tough-talking Kansans is that the state grew from a population of squatters on Indian land and pioneers who took a wrong turn along the Santa Fe Trail. As an eccentric of sorts myself, who likes in the summer to wear shorts and Hawaiian shirts in a boots and hat cow town, I stick out when picking flowers at the D & R, where most people come to put their waste to rest. Nonetheless, I'm lured there today by *Grindelia lanceolata*, more commonly known as the spiny-toothed gumweed. It's a lovely wildflower, a true specimen of evolutionary survival. As its name suggests, the gumweed has small leaves with edges like a serrated lance. Its bright yellow, flowery heads, about one and a half inches wide, protrude from a handful of secondary stems. The weed can grow as tall as three feet and can withstand cycles of excessive moisture and drought, summer heat, and hordes of ravenous insects. However, what interests me most about the gumweed is the fact that it flourishes on disturbed prairie, as does its neighbor the goldenrod. The gumweed, abundant in gravelly fields, seems well suited for life at our town dump, a natural symbol or objective correlative for what our town has become.

As I make my way over a disturbed prairie field, the soil more gravel now than good sod, Santa Fe trains make their way west though town. Emporia, true to its genesis, is still a switching yard. Almost every hour of the day and night, trains bellow through, whistling like sailors come to port. All of America—a cornucopia of commerce, global capitalism, and the American Dream—seems to roll past us: jars of pickles from Ohio in one car, heating oil in another, trailers of John Deere tractors and Ford pickups, fertilizer of nitrogen and ammonia, cars & cars & cars of coal, stacks & stacks & stacks of lumber, refrigerated boxcars of lettuce, tanks of milk or liquid propane, maybe even an entire transatlantic container filled with crates of French champagne westward bound for more glamorous locales.

While I pick my flowers, I watch the trains pass, carrying away our dreams and grain. In many respects, the American Dream, the dream of the frontier made possible by the railroad, rooted itself here on the Kansas plains. From the vast grassland, from what Anglo settlers mistook to be vacant land, from a vision of its bounty—"where the deer and the antelope play," as goes our state song—could blossom the Dream. It goes something like this: an independent, hard-working man can prosper with the grace of God and the support of his obedient wife and male children. From nothing can be made something, even something better than nature itself; the wild garden can become a cultivated one. The seemingly feral land can be tamed. As folks pushed westward for gold, space, and prosperity, they brought this dream to Kansas along the Oregon and Santa Fe trails. I've lived here long enough now to recognize that I, too, find myself at times buying into the myth, especially in a good economy with a strong demand for cut beef, radiators, soybean products, cupcakes, and dog food (all produced here in town). When there is work, our industrialists seem like benevolent gods. In a down economy, they make Emporia seem like Dickens's Coketown in *Hard Times*—"a river that ran purple with ill-smelling dye, and vast piles of building full of windows where there was a rattling and a trembling all day long, and where the piston of steam-engine worked monotonously up and down, like the head of an elephant in a state of melancholy madness.... You saw nothing in Coketown but what was severely workful." As I clip cuttings of spiny-toothed gumweed, careful not to prick my fingers, I'm reminded of the contradictions between beauty and the profane, bounty and exploitation, how in the very Bowels of Emporia, the American Dream makes its last stand. If our town had an official flower, it might appropriately be the spiny-toothed gumweed, a hint of beauty on an otherwise plain stem. On this clear blue day, as I move through the disturbed, eroded prairie field, I recognize the story of my town and what happened to the paradisal dreams of the first white settlers. Call it the Parable of the Spiny-Toothed Gumweed.

"No Styrofoam Please"

At the D & R facility, what doesn't pass by on the Santa Fe trains two hundred yards to the north gets passed here amid swarms of flies: glass; plastic of every kind, color, and shape; aluminum and tin; newspaper, junk mail, and magazines; and cardboard. My favorite machine, mostly because of its name, is the Cram-A-Lot baler, an ingenious device that compacts cardboard and newspaper into small bales that are crapped out the rear of the machine. Ask any proctologist about his work and he'll say that what gets eliminated tells more about the state of a body than anything else. What I toss out tells more about me, more about my all-American town, than I might ever have imagined.

What my town reads: *Kansas Farmer, Reader's Digest, Soap Opera Digest, Parents, Money, Kiplinger's,* the *Spiegel Catalog, Audubon, Time, U.S. News and World Report, Newsweek, Golf Digest, Home & Garden,* the *Victoria's Secret Catalog, Men's Journal, Consumer Reports, Field & Stream,* and *Midwest Living* (a favorite because it convinces Midwesterners there's something redeeming and worth celebrating in the Heartland).

What my town drinks from glass bottles: Bud Light (lots of it), Lite Beer, Gallo, Turning Leaf, Budweiser, Jack Daniels, Tanqueray, Hollandia, Krönenberg, Carlo Rossi Table Red, Elephant Malt Liquor, Corbel Canyon Chardonnay, Heineken, St. Pauli Girl.

What my town drinks from plastic bottles: anything manufactured by Coca-Cola or PepsiCo.

What my town consumes out of tin cans: Van Camp's Pork & Beans, Happy Harvest (Aldi Brand) Green Beans, Happy Harvest Kidney Beans, Happy Harvest Sweet Corn, Franco-American Meatballs, Green Giant Cut Green Beans, Best Choice Blackeye Peas, Bush's Best Pinto Beans, Ranch Style Original Texas Beans, Golden Sound Basil Seed Drink (I wish I saw who drank that).

From the looks of the overflowing bins, we're a very average American town with little diversity of interest in our reading, comestibles, and taste. I had expected more surprises, perhaps a look at desires more secret than what townsfolk surreptitiously order from Victoria's Secret. I also noticed we're a heavy-drinking town, which most people would never admit to in a place where three out of the nine pages in the phone book's C section are churches. We also drink far too many soft drinks. Perhaps my biggest discovery is the ingenuity of our plastics, countless variously shaped and sized containers that truly attest to our American creativity and inventiveness (in fact, my own grandfather played a key role in the development of the squeezable plastic bottle that has saved us all from terrible waits for our ketchup).

"Types of Waste Accepted"

Picking flowers at the dump has its advantages; I get to watch a lot of strange people come and go. As I've discovered in our town, as in life, it's important to know what you can and cannot eliminate, so it pays to notice the sign at the dump's entrance, not far from the field where I stand with a handful of gumweed: "Types of Waste Accepted: Residential Waste—Dismounted Tires—Commercial Waste—Yard Waste—Construction Demolition Waste." For a moment, I wonder what is not accepted, but there is a sign for that, too. "Types of Waste Not Accepted: Medical Waste—Animal Waste—Liquid Waste." But the rules seem fuzzy; will they take commercial animal waste or does the "animal" in the "waste" override the "commercial," and what about hybrid waste like the dead possum in the street outside my apartment complex? I raise this question to the attendant, who gives me an odd look of misunderstanding then points to the sign. "These are the kinds of stuff we take," he says. The authorities at the D & R facility field such inquiries very seriously, as seriously as I ponder misplaced commas and sentence fragments in my freshman composition class. On one level, it's reassuring to know they care, as long as you do not ask complex questions or use the word *hybrid*. I should also point out that at the entrance to our dump is a stoplight run by another attendant in a small booth to which is attached an air conditioner (does it eliminate the cesspool stench from across the street or pump it in?). Like an Eastern European border guard, the attendant regulates traffic in and out of the dump. While I admire the efficiency, I am struck by the need for the traffic signal. There are only some twenty-five thousand people in our town far away from any major city, and most of these people I never see at the D & R facility. I am, however, confident that waste not suitable to one of the well-stated criteria will not be smuggled into our dump, which, I hasten to point out again, is just across from the highly toxic and highly guarded slaughterhouse cesspools. While the dump and its guard are impressive, from the looks of things around town, it seems most waste either winds up along the roadway, beside a porch, stacked in a garage, sold as antiques to tourists, or piled in somebody's backyard auto garden, where old cars rust back to a mineral state.

As I stop to cut another stem of gumweed, careful not to prick my fingers, I spy the traffic coming and going from the yard. Everybody gets through the crossing without a hassle, unlike the Tijuana–San Diego border where cars are regularly screened in a secondary search facility. Although our town is zealous enough to regulate the nonexistent traffic into its dump, there are no facilities for a secondary search, if the need arose, perhaps to catch hybrid-waste smugglers. Years ago, when I lived in San Diego and traveled frequently to Mexico for cheap entertainment—because I regard this piece as a family essay, I will not elaborate—I was stopped plenty of times at the border, not by Mexican *Federales* but by the American Border Patrol. Friendly *Federales*, unlike their American counterparts, wave you into Mexico with a smile, as if Americans have nothing worth smuggling across our southern neighbor's border. I've tried on occasion to figure out why I'm frequently stopped at borders—strip-searched in Tecate, another time probed at length about guns when traveling into Canada, detained in the former Communist Yugoslavia, questioned in Switzerland. Perhaps I fit the smuggler's profile, whatever that may be— longish hair, olive-toned skin, a smart-ass smile, cynical quips, the earring, especially the earring. Be it our dump or a foreign country, I get so paranoid about crossing borders that I avoid them at all costs. I'm not worried about myself—I once had to explain to Canadian authorities (another trip north) that my traveler's diarrhea pills were just that: "Take one," I said, "and let me know in the morning." They didn't find me funny, then persisted to question me for two hours about every unmarked medicine in my small plastic safety-locked bottle: airsickness pill, stomach acid blocker, sleeping aid, generic (unmarked) sinus antihistamines, generic Sudafed, generic vitamin C, generic zinc tablets, generic aspirin, generic Tylenol, and generic ibuprofen (in case you're wondering, I'm cheap and get lots of headaches. Let me also point out that each pill does something different and, taken in combination, can cure just about any debility from which I've ever suffered). While they were initially convinced I was unfit to enter Canada, where I could possibly contaminate the northern gene pool, they eventually permitted me entrance with the declaration that I would return to the States, where my types properly belonged, within a week.

Entry into our dump is much easier. On this day, folks on the inside stop at a large pile of discarded bricks near the entry gate. I watch some placing a number of these bricks in their trunks. Not until I get home do I discover that it's not the popularity of brick patios this summer that attracts people to the pile, but a chance at recovering a piece of our town's history. The bricks come from our former train depot, a building fallen recently to arsonists (what a blaze it was!). Though the depot hadn't seen trains for years, folks in the town remembered it with nostalgia, that pain of memory. My octogenarian neighbor, an accomplished amateur photographer who takes pictures even now with advanced Parkinson's that blurs all his shots, has fond memories of the depot. He's lived his entire life in Emporia, except for a brief stint in the Army during World War Two. To him, the depot is a metaphor for life's transitions. In the old days, as he calls them, the only way in or out of town for those without vehicles was by foot or train. This man came home from the war on the train, took a train trip for his honeymoon, and rode the train on weekends to Kansas City. The passing of the depot is the passing of his era, each brick a piece of a fractured memory from a time before the town sold out to industry (*Right on!* I hear Edward Abbey cheer me).

"Random Waste Screening Is Practiced Here"

I've said it once and I'll say it again: whatever we are as a town can be found at the dump where I pick my spiny-toothed gumweed. When I first came to town for a job interview at its small state teacher's college, somehow they managed to avoid showing me this corner of prairie paradise. I wanted to believe it was a casual oversight but have since realized there is an unspoken rule, flower lover or not, to refrain from driving any prospective candidate past the slaughterhouse, behind which is located the D & R facility with all its spiny-toothed gumweed for the taking. When the town or college has visitors, we talk about our glorious past, the rise of the cattle and oil industries, and the years of William Allen White, our Pulitzer Prize–winning journalist. Before coming to Emporia, I'd never heard of White, but in Emporia, the White family legacy lives on: there is the White self-guided driving tour, the White house, the White memorial, the White library, the White Auditorium, and White's *Gazette* with daily reports on county prison meals (Tonight's meal for 62 men, 13 women: Corn dogs, tater tots, five-way vegetables, pudding, coffee/tea. Saturday night's meal for 66 men, 10 women: Tacos, refried beans, corn, cake, coffee/tea). Whenever anybody mentioned White during my initial visit, I made sure to give a requisite nod of approval, so as not to appear as ignorant as I really was. However, after I took the job, I made sure to check into White's history. The more I learned, the more, like my octogenarian neighbor, I found myself longing for the good old days when, according to White, small-town Kansas voiced the concerns of a nation. It's hard to imagine a time when Kansans wielded so much influence (in fairness, I must mention we are the home state of Dwight and Milton Eisenhower, William Inge, William Stafford, and Bob Dole). As went Kansas, White was fond of saying, so went the nation.

White even built his own version of Never, Never Land here, our Peter Pan Park on the south edge of town with its fairy-tale themes, allusions to classical architecture, monkey house (demolished years ago), children's pool, and cultivated gardens grown upon what was once river bottomland. White wanted his park to be reflective of the ideals of our prospering town, an image of the dreams possible to achieve. The park, like the dump, is now in a degraded state, its concrete bandstand crumbling, the reflecting pond filled with sediment and algae, trees and shrubs growing unpruned, the lawn going to seed each summer. On the outskirts of the park live our town's silent minority, the slaughterhouse's migrant workers. Not long after I moved to town, people warned me about the park and told me not to walk there alone.

"Gibbons Recycling and Scrap Metal"

If I were to continue walking through this field and if I could climb a ten-foot barbed-wire fence topped with razor-sharp coil, the kind found at places like Leavenworth Federal Penitentiary, I would find the answers to the questions I have raised, though I can already smell them when the wind blows north over the IBP wastewater lagoons across the road. Next to the D & R facility and field of gumweed is a salvage yard, the kind complete with a vicious dog to protect, I assume, the junk. In the years I've been driving past the yard, the junk seems to be accumulating faster than the owner sells it. Perhaps the price of scrap can't compete with the ease of extracting raw materials from pristine places (*Right on!*).

A small list (or what I see from a safe distance): rusting refrigerators without doors (which is reassuring since no bodies can be stuffed inside), washers and dryers dating from the Nixon administration, broken farm implements we didn't send to Russia or Africa, metal oxygen canisters, rusting barbecue grills, crumpled guttering, stoves from the Eisenhower years, car wheels, car bumpers (from when they used to be metal), car frames, skeletal patio umbrellas, and an overturned wheelchair.

A refresher list of what surrounds the D & R: the IBP slaughterhouse and Santa Fe lines to the north, the IBP cesspools and tallgrass prairie to the south, Peter Pan Park and the Latino neighborhoods to the southeast, the Gibbons scrap yard and Duffers Driving Range down the street.

Put these lists together and what you have is a metaphor for the failure of White's dream of Emporia, his American garden. What White wanted, as becomes clear from his many writings, was a pastoral community with burgeoning industrial growth, the kind of county seat envisioned by our forefathers Arthur Barlowe, William Byrd, William Bartram, and Thomas Jefferson (this is the point where I would teach my students about paradoxes). Time and time again, as our zoning laws here make clear—grain elevators or a slaughterhouse across the street from single-family housing; a driving range without protective netting adjacent to a road; an interstate abutting the backyards of our town's most expensive housing, if you can believe, in the two-hundred-thousand-dollar range—the town has catered to industry for its survival. Even our streets are named for the worker and his dream: Commercial, Merchant, Exchange, Industrial, and Union (although there are no unions here). Nonetheless, what we are as Americans comes from our town, our blood and sweat, the tobacco spit of our migrant workers: beef, dessert cakes, radiators, truck engines, ice scrapers, pet food.

Where there was once the dream of quiet streets near a pastoral park, there is now an omnipresent industrial din, the grind and low moans of Santa Fe trains, and the sound of traffic whizzing by along I-35 at all hours of the day and night (I can hear the noise in my apartment with the windows closed and can only imagine what our landed gentry along the interstate hear in their living rooms, a thought that gives me immense pleasure). The town went awry when it catered to industry to provide jobs for our locals, but nobody foresaw that these factories would import their own cheap, union-free labor from Latin America, twenty-five percent of our town's population (these numbers are even higher in western Kansas). While Latinos are our workforce, they sadly make up a tiny percentage of Emporia State University's largely homogeneous student population. And most of the wages these factories penuriously dole out to our foreign workers leave the town and country via Western Union. The rest go either to Wal-Mart or, with those who brave the tollway, to places like Wichita, Topeka, Lawrence, or Kansas City. Whenever I complain about our town's many noxious odors, I'm quickly reminded, "It's the smell of money!" But to me it's more like the smell of rot, the death of a town that has become an indentured servant through its Faustian pact with industry (*Right on!*).

"The Driving Range: A Vision"

With an armful of gumweed, goldenrod, and pollen-rich sunflowers, I drive off toward home in my thirteen-year-old Ford Escort. I leave behind the D & R facility, see the noxious cesspools fade from view, and watch the junkyard dog bark viciously at my car as another Santa Fe train rolls into, then out of, town. After passing the grain elevator, I wave to a gray-haired woman picking up golf balls by hand in a field of hard-packed dirt at Duffers Driving Range.

The range is a new business on a weedy field in the shadow of the IBP slaughterhouse. To the west of the range are the IBP soccer fields (dirt fields) built for the migrant workers. A sign adjacent to the range outlines the rules for the field's use. I like number 5, "No Fighting (No Peleas)," as if these foreign workers would emulate American sports etiquette. The operators of the driving range, an elderly couple of chain smokers who work out of a smoke-filled shack the size of two outhouses, have yet to purchase a tractor to retrieve golf balls; instead, they courageously, or stupidly, walk the field themselves to retrieve balls, even while golfers are still hitting. The couple symbolizes America's entrepreneurial spirit, the optimism expressed in the very notion that they can retrieve by hand all those balls scattered like hail, or dreams, across the barren field. I like to believe the old couple's hope will last long enough for the balls they retrieve to add up to a proper tractor. When I pass, there are a few duffers whacking balls at the old lady and toward my car. I honk and give them the finger as I drive by.

Under the influence of the aromatic flowers on the empty seat beside me, I have a vision: a golf course with manicured, chemical-free fairways (*Right on!*), a new American garden covering what was once the Bowels of Emporia, a gentrification above all gentrifications. There are sparkling ponds, water holes where the cesspools once were. There are pruned trees and decorative shrubs along the fairways. There are businessmen in slacks playing a few rounds with their caddies; they've come from Kansas City and Wichita for a quiet day in the country. The former slaughterhouse workers, now unionized, run the club owned by the town; they receive stock options with their generous paychecks. Their families live in the new housing developments overlooking the lake along the eighteenth hole. With revenues from the course, they've built a new monkey house at Peter Pan Park, where blue emergency call boxes have been affixed to the stately trunks of towering elms. The university flourishes, too. Students can't wait to come to a college with a world-class golf course—a design even more astonishing in scope than the Colbert Hills course carved from the Kanza Prairie near Kansas State University in Manhattan—and because of the impact of Tiger Woods, there's even a rising diversity of faces both on campus and on the course. There is a sign, too, over the paved driveway to the clubhouse, "Peter Pan

Public Golf Club," to properly commemorate William Allen White's legacy and vision. The large clubhouse doors can be opened by pulling the bronzed cast handles of spiny-toothed gumweed. Inside the club, the large glass windows in the lounge give players a commanding view of the last preserved fields of prairie tallgrass with their blooming wildflowers of tall goldenrod and burr marigold that wave in a fresh south wind. Emporia makes it to the top of the list of *100 Best Small Towns in America* and is regularly featured on the Golf Channel. When it's my turn to tee off, I check my grip, take a few practice swings, then whack the ball westward. Of course, it's a glorious shot, sailing forth gracefully and landing out of sight somewhere far down the middle of the green fairway. When I hop into my cart to go find my ball, my caddie, a former stripper from Cabaret U.S.A., hands me a cold beer and tells me about my wonderful stroke. It's a good life, I think, another beautiful day for the links.

EPIPHANIA

Well, they say that Santa Fe is less than ninety miles away
And I got time to roll a number and rent a car ...

So I'll stop when I can, find some fried eggs and country ham
I'll find somewhere where they don't care who I am.

—Neil Young, "Albuquerque"

At some point, something was going to happen. That much was certain.

As we climbed into the Alamo shuttle that would take us to our car, I felt a prescience the way my hip bone tells me it will rain. I had a similar feeling last fall when I had come to know before it happened that the sky would fill with waves of blackbirds. Sure enough, a few afternoons later I had stood with my daughter in a recess between two cottonwoods as the birds passed over us like dark water. I was certain as the shuttle drove away from the airport that something similar was about to happen again. A brief moment would open, pour itself into another, then another, unfolding and expanding perhaps something like space itself, or the forces in an A-bomb's mushroom cloud moments after detonation. That's how much I knew upon arrival, but I couldn't say when.

Maybe the billboard on Gibson Boulevard just down the road from the Albuquerque International Sunport triggered such feelings, at least the start of them—"Welcome to New Mexico: America's Nuclear Weapons Colony." Then again, maybe it was my travel companion, Mr. Tecate Man, a graduate student of mine at the college—whose identity I'll keep anonymous for his own good—who convinced me to stop our rental so he could snap a photo of the sign with his camera-in-a-box.

In a stream of heavy mid-afternoon traffic, I pulled over our forest green Buick Century, a boat of a car that made us look more like government investigators than Kansas academics heading to an early spring conference on popular culture. Because we looked like agents in our blue conference blazers and dark sunglasses, nobody wanted to appear too interested in what we were doing; then again, perhaps everyone had grown immune to the sign, lost in the city's billboard pollution. I wanted to tell Mr. Tecate Man what I knew, how something would happen and that he should be prepared, but I didn't yet know where the signs were pointing. Maybe what would manifest itself had nothing to do with him; then again, maybe it had everything to do with him—I couldn't be certain. "Be careful," I warned, as he unbuckled his seat belt.

After he stepped out of the car, he stood in front of the sign, dwarfed by its enormity. He was in his element, a pop-culture buff drawn to eccentricities—books on gravesite memorials, totems in rural Kansas, folk art and folk songs. With a few beers in him, he might sing folk favorites such as "The Farmer Is the Man" or "The Kansas Fool"—*Oh! Kansas fool! Poor Kansas fool! / The banker makes of you a tool.* He could even tell you where in Kansas you might find the World's Largest Ball of Twine, the World's Largest Hand-Dug Well, or the Barbed Wire Museum. As I watched him line up the tiny viewfinder of his disposable camera, I tried not to worry about the billboard's shaking in the wind. I was uneasy at best, knowing what I knew about that something I couldn't predict. Perhaps I would come to know in explosive moments resembling fission something about myself, maybe something about Mr. Tecate Man, perhaps a thing or two about this city, its past, something essential about this desert place. So I waited for whatever would come my way with the hope that, in whatever fell upon us, there would be knowing.

The expensive billboard, I was certain, begged to be understood—portent, omen, presage—a maximum resonance of conflicting signs. Its "Welcome" seemed innocuous enough for a tourist town, and "America" played up what patriotism I should have despite being in New Mexico, the once-disputed territory ceded in the Treaty of Guadalupe Hidalgo after an offensive war, a state with lands (and people) later considered disposable enough to test atomic explosions. The phrase "Nuclear Weapons Colony" was, however, quite discomforting and ambiguous at best. Was it irony? Who was the colonizer of this colony? Should we have packed Geiger counters and protective eyewear? Watching Mr. Tecate Man shoot the billboard like a model for a swimsuit calendar, I thought, not unfittingly, of the allusive Hart Crane: *Going west—young man ... science—COMMERCE and the HOLYGHOST ... So the 20th Century.* Then came to me explosive fragments of Eliot: *After the agony in stony places ... Rock and no water and the sandy road ... There is not even silence in the mountains.* Maybe this is where I first felt something significant, an inkling of things to come, a desire for coherence in what surfaced.

"Get back in the car," I shouted over the traffic. "One shot is enough." It was a phrase I'd use again later when we closed down our hotel bar on the last night of the conference. Nevertheless, he insisted on taking a few more photos.

"Just in case," he yelled back.

"In case of what?"

"In case something happens," he said.

"What could happen?"

"Anything," he shouted. "Anything at all."

In a strange way, only moments after finishing my ham sandwich and the remainder of my bottled Kansas water on the Alamo shuttle, driven by a bowler named Vincent with a respectable 196 average, Mr. Tecate Man made sense, more sense than he usually made in the entire three hours of my seminar on twentieth-century poetry. Of course I'm being facetious here. It was as if he could read my mind, knew what pressed to be known. Despite the veracity of his sobriquet, Mr. Tecate Man was one of my brightest students. The way he traveled without wrinkling the clothes that he stuffed into his book bag was itself testament to the magic of the mostly clean-shaven man, who sported a tuft of beard at the tip of his chin resembling something on a billy goat. In mutual jest, he liked to tell me, I could, in the right clothes, pass for a trucker because of my "mullet," a length of hair at the back of my neck longer and in disproportion to the curls on the top of my head. "It's a term," he said, "the origins to be found in the discourse of interstate service stations." I'd supervised enough of his research to grant him this small breach of professional respect; besides, he understood my fondness for etymology, especially the lingo of the American road warrior. If I looked like a mullet-sporting trucker, I fancied it a compliment, especially in our effeminate profession of literary study, where men in pastel sweaters often have hands softer than their wives' butts.

When Mr. Tecate Man hopped back into the Buick, I felt a tinge of relief, a momentary ease from my recent edginess, those *obscure reveries / Of the inward gaze*, as Pound might have put it. Our Odyssey begun, we drove off toward the heart of downtown Albuquerque to rooms, separate rooms thankfully, at the Old Town Sheraton. In my younger days as a graduate student of limited means, I would have welcomed sharing a room with a reveler like Mr. Tecate Man, but I've grown to appreciate my own accommodations, courtesy of university travel funds, which each year the state threatens to cut further. As we drove along, we anticipated how we'd spend back-breaking, mind-numbing hours listening to the latest research in our fields from some of the most remarkable scholars in the country, myself included, I must add. At the end of our long days, after listening to panel after panel, after filling our minds to capacity with erudite learning, we'd feel wholly drained, perhaps only able to mumble something similar to *ga, ga, goo*. We'd hear the droners and pontificators, confront the ubiquitous conference pit bulls and badgers, but in all fairness, we'd listen to a number of engaging speakers, whom I knew deserved much more pay than they were getting in salary and travel.

Then there was the seamier side of the event—the gambling, pickups and affairs, people who spent their entire trip in the hotel pub or in their rooms watching in-house soft porn, cheap thrills with titles like *Nasty Nurses I & II* or *Principal Seductions*. Our hotel, I would discover, was no different with its similarly enticing titles, a poetry of lust and fantasy, a humor of incredulous hyperbole and uncommon feats: *Just Filthy Sex— Gonzo Edition, Sexmates of My Wife, Copulation/Portraits in Blue Double Feature, Wild Thing V.I.P. Cut, Intense Sex, Dream Quest Special Feature, Raw Talent/Sex Slave Double Feature,* and, if those weren't already over the top, the promisingly satiating *Sexual Indulgence.*

Onward to the pleasure dome, we zipped through light traffic, something similar to L.A.'s on Saturday morning, up I-25 toward the I-40 junction turnoff toward Old Town. For those who have never traveled to Albuquerque, a.k.a. in local-speak, "Burque" (pronounced búr-kay), the land can seem surprisingly desiccated, even for a desert. I'm always struck here by the brownness of everything, including the buildings, as if all were camouflaged to avoid being seen by passing aircraft. At first glance, Burque resembles something of the mythic West turned modern metropolitan pueblo, an odd mix of celebration and repudiation toward its colonial histories. As I swerved to avoid a tumbleweed in the middle of my lane, Simon Ortiz's "Sand Creek" popped into my head: *This America*, he writes, *has been a burden / of steel and mad / death*. The landscape surrounding Duke City, spaces suitable for John Wayne, John Ford, and Leslie Silko, is overwhelming and vast, the hills and mountains monumental, especially to somebody from the Plains like myself. To the west, the gentle, pointed volcanic slopes of the Petroglyph National Monument rise from brown mesas to meet the blue horizon. To the northeast, the Manzanita Mountains and Sandia Peak cast morning shadows over the city, through whose center flow the cool waters of the Rio Grande river. The Santa Fe Trail, which passes just north of where I live in Kansas, ends about an hour or so up I-25 in Santa Fe. To the south, there's the vast American desert, an area believed safe enough to test atomic bombs, a desolate place with names like Jornada del Muerto (Journey of the Dead) and a town called Truth or Consequences. If something explosive were going to happen, this would be the place for it.

As I drove, Mr. Tecate Man snapped photos, some with the window rolled down and others with his small camera pressed to the windshield. When he wished to photograph me, I protested vehemently. "Come on, man, just one shot," he repeated until I gave in. While he photographed me in a flurry of shots from various angles, I thought, as three older Ford Broncos rumbled past, how Albuquerque must be the Ford Bronco Capital of the World, or at least where Broncos came to retire once people like O. J. Simpson needed a newer model. The character of most any city, I am certain, can be defined by its most common mode of transportation. In New York, the rapid transportation of subways defines the hurry of a New York minute; in Chicago, the elevated train harkens back nostalgically to the city's past of bootlegging gangsters and afternoon baseball; Los Angeles has smoggy freeways for its sporty convertibles that reflect the casual SoCal style, American individuality gone out of control on congested roadways.

After another old Bronco rumbled past us, I turned to Mr. Tecate Man. "Snap a photo of the next one for our friends back home," my friends, of course, traveling in a different circle than his. As a courtesy, Mr. Tecate Man rolled his window back down to take a couple of surreptitious shots while I, as inconspicuously as possible, sidled our Century up to the sun-faded truck in front of us for a close-up. *Why not, buy a goddam big car,* Creeley might have said if traveling with us.

"I'll send you the developing bill," Mr. Tecate Man joked, turning the film advance gear with his index finger.

"Try something fancy. Shoot the next one from the side view mirror," I suggested, but instead Mr. Tecate Man started to photograph the road workers as we slowed down for some construction.

Fifteen minutes of driving through Burque with only a minor delay for roadwork, I felt like we had gone nowhere—maybe it was only my mind circling within itself seeking for a way, if it were possible, to string these signs together. The city sprawled around us, streets crisscrossing the valley in neat parallel lines. Everything from the dry hard dirt to the adobe buildings seemed the same wherever we went. "We need beer," Mr. Tecate Man suggested, breaking the monotony, "for our rooms." Staring out at dryness itself, I couldn't help but think that I was traveling with a man of potential genius, let alone that I had an insatiable thirst since polishing off my water and salty ham sandwich on the Alamo shuttle. Considering hotel bar prices, especially the in-room minibar, it was a good idea to stock up. There are few greater pleasures in the world, for the married or unmarried, than being sprawled across the raft of a king-size hotel mattress—the kind of bed that gets more action in a month than most of us see in a lifetime—a cool brew in one hand, the cable remote in the other.

At the turnoff following our hotel exit at the I-40 and I-25 junction, where we could have turned north to Billings, Montana, or east to Wilmington, North Carolina, I headed south. Unable to find a liquor store, I pulled into the parking lot of a bar advertising its drive-up package service. Here that prescient feeling, this time a déjà vu of sorts, returned to me again, as if at any moment the something I waited for might happen. I felt like we were in the wrong place at the wrong time, though it was difficult to say for certain. I followed a faded yellow line to the tavern's back door where hung a chalkboard noting the daily specials, Budweiser $6.96, Miller Lite $6.96, Coors $6.96. Everything except Smirnoff vodka was $6.96, the Smirnoff seeming out of place in this tequila town. Perhaps it was the drive-up service that triggered something in me. By no means was this the first drive-up tavern I'd ever visited; they're common across western states like Arizona and Nevada, where open roads in the desert are meant for drinking and driving and shooting road signs, or at least they used to be before too many people drove off cliffs, into cacti, or into other people.

As we were contemplating our order, I anticipated the appearance of a man with long dark hair, a bushy mustache, and blue tattoos on his arms, somebody who might reveal something to me. We waited but nothing happened—no man, no service, nothing, a false vision. "They think we're agents," I told Mr. Tecate Man, "FBI, City Health, ATF, maybe Vice. It's our car."

"You think so?"

"Sure," I told him. "Add it up, our green Century rental, our dark glasses and blue blazers."

"Never thought of it."

"That's why I'm the professor," I said.

"Piled High and Deep. Perhaps you should honk, just maybe they're inside leaning on pool cues with the juke on loud."

"Maybe. But the prices are a bit steep. I'm on a fixed per diem," I reminded him. "Let's cruise a bit more, see what we find. I had a bad feeling about this place when we pulled up. There's no sense waiting for something like bullets to fly."

"You've got a crazy imagination," he reminded me.

"It's not so much in my mind," I tried to explain. "It's a vibe I've been getting since we landed."

"A what?"

"A vibe."

"You don't believe in such things, do you?"

We pulled back onto the dusty street in Thirst Country where scrub cactus grew around the bus stops, then drove past a sprawl of businesses—heavy equipment rental, Mexican restaurant, Indian jewelry shop, tattoo parlor. Before any Broncos with fringe in the rear window rumbled by again, we found ourselves at an Albertson's supermarket. Inside the market, the bright lights gave the produce a sparkling glow. The oranges looked so good they seemed fake, the apples so red they had to be painted, the Anaheim chilies wonderfully green in their twisted phallic shapes—*What thoughts I have of you tonight, Walt Whitman … Are you my Angel?* Unlike Kansas where Sunkist and Dole (not Bob and Elizabeth) send their unworthy produce to the meat and potatoes crowd, I knew here the cashiers of Burque could properly identify an artichoke or tell the difference between parsley and cilantro. The supermarket demonstrated in its incomparable display of produce a respect for food akin to Los Angeles with its proliferation of giant groceries and eateries, where corner taco shacks are as common as bars in Milwaukee or the once-ubiquitous family-owned pizza joints in Chicago.

In the beer section, with its row of refrigerators two feet taller than me, I grabbed a six-pack of Coors, a dollar cheaper than at the drive-up tavern. When out West, Rocky Mountain pisswater, as it is more commonly called, takes on a special appeal. Perhaps it's nostalgia; I associate the beer with an old bootlegging neighbor who smuggled Coors in his station wagon across state lines on every family ski trip in the days before national distribution. Then again, it reminds me of my teenage road trips across the West, where in the back of my buddy's Jeep, we drank 3.2 Coors, then lined the roll bar with our empties, even in Utah, and somehow survived.

"When in Rome," Mr. Tecate Man shouted, "drink Tecate." Under each arm, he carried a twelve-pack, one for each of us. Looking at him making his way up the aisle, I had a brief vision of things to come, a brief unraveling of how he would forever be known as Mr. Tecate Man.

On Saturday night in downtown Burque, we would be in a theater along Central, old Route 66. We would be mesmerized by Stanley Jordan's guitar playing, as if he'd bargained for his talent at a crossroads. At approximately 9:52 p.m. Standard Mountain Time, Mr. Tecate Man would lean back to attempt to tell me something, then plummet from his barstool to the sticky floor, spilling his Tecate on a man in a black leather jacket behind him. It would be an uncomfortable moment, the leather-jacket man contemplating bludgeoning Mr. Tecate Man as he mopped himself off with a handful of drink napkins. The tension would rise until Mr. Tecate Man, acting diplomatically, would agree to buy the man-in-leather a new drink to ease tensions.

Such a brief vision of things to come nearly made me forget I was still standing in the beer aisle. I was unsure of how much time had passed. I had come over the course of my life to believe it is possible to escape time. Ever since I was a young boy, whole moments seemed to open themselves up to me, states of heightened consciousness, deep perception, scaffolding time. To a boy, these were more than simple daydreams; I often seemed transported, to where or what I can't definitively say. Then there came the day at age twelve when I was hit by a car while riding my bicycle. After the impact, which hurled me some twenty feet, I found myself disembodied for a time, hovering over my fractured self on the pavement where others had gathered about me. Such strange, recurring experiences might have led to my commitment in a mental institution had I not read Vladimir Nabokov's *Speak, Memory*, where he likens his deeply engaged, atemporal perceptions to having passed into a "fissure." "A poet," he goes on, "must have the capacity of thinking several things at a time." From Nabokov, I learned to trust my insight, to open myself up to time's fissures, the planes of a moment, heightened perception. Maybe it was the grocery store's fluorescent lights whose vibrating frequencies always make me uneasy, but something soon would manifest itself, something powerful and strange, that much I knew. I had to remain in a state of elevated awareness for what might happen.

At the checkout, we showed the cashier our IDs, received the obligatory refrain, "You're not in Kansas anymore," then paid for our beer. Outside, wherever I looked, people appeared to be drinking things in their cars, or maybe that's just how it seems when you are dying for something to quench your thirst in the desert. On the entire ride to our hotel, I fought back the temptation to crack open a cold one. At least I was not setting a bad example for the kid, I thought, until I looked down to see an open can in Mr. Tecate Man's lap.

"Where'd that come from?" I asked.

"Maybe you should keep your eyes on the road instead of on my crotch," he told me.

"Don't flatter yourself, " I said, "and duck down." The rest of the ride all that could be seen of Mr. Tecate Man was the very top of his head, that is, unless you were rumbling past in a Bronco with high clearance. I knew then, too, how so many beer cans and empty bottles came to line the shoulders of our great highways, enough of them to pick up for a second income.

Back at the Sheraton, after a necessary change of rooms to accommodate my requested nonsmoking quarters—not recently smoked in, that is—I found my new digs as luxurious as expected for a convention hotel with lots of foot traffic. The new room (and the requisite second tipping of the bellboy) seemed better, too, once housekeeping showed up to clean the bathroom and remove the soiled towels that had apparently been overlooked earlier in the day's service. All in all, the raft of a bed had just enough support, the carpet and bathroom seemed clean enough, and the mass-produced prints of cacti above the headboard were not half bad for hotel wall art. However, the view from the seventh floor of warehouses and parking lots paled by comparison to the view of Old Town's San Felipe de Neri church that could be seen like an omen from my first room's windows.

After housekeeping cleaned up, I put the Tecate on ice and poured myself a tequila from my room's minibar (a costly but prudent $6.50 decision). Then I flipped through the fourteen cable channels, nearly five times my own three freebies back home, not including PBS, which I get on clear days, if the wind is right. After three minutes of CNN and at least ten of the Weather Channel, six of which were commercials, the hotel porn began to look inviting, even if it seemed like a guilty pleasure (no pun intended) in the late afternoon. Instead, I settled on watching the Weather Channel repeat the forecast some more until a calm came over me unlike anything throughout the day. Maybe it was the region's Rocky Mountain winter storm warning that put me at ease, knowing that in Burque there was only a slim chance for rain. I half expected such a forecast in toting along my umbrella at my wife's urging. "It never rains in the desert," I had told her.

All matter of the universe, I thought as I rose after nodding off during the pollen count report, *tends toward rest unless otherwise acted upon by force.* It was an old theorem from a college physics class that popped into my head from time to time. As I opened a well-chilled Tecate and watched the weather again for the storm front's progression, I decided to leave early for dinner, where I was to share a meal with Mr. Tecate Man and this philosopher we met in the hotel lobby upon arriving.

Outside the air was still dry, though cooler than earlier in the day, with a slight breeze. Before my dinner rendezvous, I took a detour into a few Old Town shops on San Felipe Plaza to find a keepsake for my wife. I surveyed display after display of turquoise jewelry and overpriced pottery; expensive hand-woven rugs; desert-themed prints from Georgia O'Keeffe, Gorman's Indians, and countless landscapes of New Mexico scrub brush; made-in-China magnets of adobe pueblos, faux Indian wall hangings, and plastic cactus ornaments; ashtrays where you could rub out a cigarette on the flag of New Mexico; souvenir shot glasses and spoons; bumper stickers and patches; lacquered red chili ristras, chili magnets, chili salt and pepper shakers, plastic chili wall decorations, and chili powder to go; and postcards of saints, Hollywood cowboys, and Indians, including Plains tribal chiefs who never set foot in the desert. Under the influence of this cornucopia of commerce, I bought two things I didn't need and shipped them home: a turquoise bracelet for my wife that she would never wear because she doesn't like to wear jewelry, and a crooked black clay pot that looked far more properly proportioned in the shop's dim lighting than it ever has on our bookshelf. If I hadn't had to meet with Mr. Tecate Man and the philosopher, I probably would have also bought a chili pepper hot plate that I had admired for some time, even though it would have never made it out of our kitchen drawer.

Since I had stepped into the shops, the wind had picked up. The sun too had begun to set, giving a glow to the busy plaza. On my way to the restaurant, I took a detour to see the Madonna and Child carved by Toby Avila into a crooked cottonwood tree in the San Felipe de Neri church's parking lot, a *tiptoe into one of the side streets*, à la Ashbery. Though tour books date the church structure to 1793, and the founding of the church in 1706, no books note the carving that I'd heard about from my folk-art hero, Mr. Tecate Man.

Tucked behind the back of the church, the tall tree had grown thick with age, its bark deeply furrowed. As much as I recall about what happened at this moment, I especially remember the quiet, as if the traffic had somehow disappeared, the world put on pause. The wind from the approaching front blew about the budding branches of the tree's canopy. In a dull light cast out from the church's windows, I stared at the carving, at the Madonna's gentle face filled with an ineffable peace. To her breast she clutched her small child, who seemed satiated with an inexhaustible love. The artist, too, in seeking to share such a vision, must have known something about this mother-love that gives the simple carving its beauty. To look at the carving was to peer into the exposed heart of the tree, at the miracle of its center that gave the cottonwood its life. It was an overpowering metaphor, especially when I thought about how I clutched my own baby daughter with so much love and fear. The shrine so moved me, I decided to dust off a few decades-old prayers. It was tough going at first to recall the words, the forgotten difficulty of what I once called faith, but slowly these old words surfaced as if they'd never left, the way thick cottonwood roots bring up deep water in a desert. I chanted, unsure to whom or what I was petitioning, as if prayer itself were a song that alone fortified. As I continued, I thought about the vacancy of doubt, and its necessity, in order to believe in anything so beautiful as mother and child.

Above the tree, a flock of pigeons suddenly lifted from the church's roof, then began to circle. Around and around they flew, the flock gathering in number. The birds seemed like shadows against the darkening sky as they moved round and round. I knew then, remembering my earlier experience with blackbirds, that from the moment the pigeons took flight, the something I had anticipated since landing had begun. A fissure of sorts had opened. I glanced up at the birds in the wan light as they twisted and turned, lifted and sank, their wings beating out a code in their flutter.

The next thing I knew I was eating chili rellenos with beans and rice in an Old Town cantina with Mr. Tecate Man and our philosopher. *Awareness,* I thought, *awareness.* While a teen beauty with hair like licorice and eyes like almonds served us Dos Equis, the philosopher was doing all the talking, telling us about phenomenology, which he could barely pronounce because he'd been drinking. I wanted to ask him about fissures, about faith, about how knowing manifests itself, but I didn't want to disturb the equilibrium of his rant. Needing a cigarette, he said, Mr. Tecate Man excused himself from our table to go buy a pack of Marlboros, leaving me alone with our guest, who kept on talking even though I wasn't really listening. Instead, I was staring at a singed picture of Gloria Estefan above the cash register wondering if she too had had the chili rellenos, which weren't as good as I had expected.

As the philosopher droned on, I wanted to know if the piñata above our table was filled with candy, then I imagined kids swinging blindly until the belly of this lamb spilled open to release whatever was inside. For some reason, I felt sorry for the lamb caught up in the piñata's ritual sacrifice; each violent swing, the darkness inside of us transformed into a shower of candy. The Mexican *canción* creating the cantina's ambience made me further wonder if the giant mural of Cortés on the adjacent wall was revered or despised.

As the song cried on about love gone bad, suddenly I felt sad and lonely, with half a plate of uneaten food I couldn't bring myself to finish. *Could the carved Madonna save a sinner like me?* Though I hadn't been to a church service in a decade or to confession in more than half a lifetime, so moved was I from the shrine and birds that I had gone into the church to make a donation and three wishes for my family. Votive candles burned brightly from the corners of the chapel as I eased myself down on a wooden kneeler at the back. Except for an old woman draped in a black shawl sitting near the altar, I was alone. In this hollow chamber, I felt as if I could hear my own heart;

certainly, I could hear my own breathing. The inside of the chapel seemed somehow a metaphor for the inside of the body, a patchwork of shadows against whose darkness candles brightly burned. I wondered for a moment what it was I believed in or seemed always to be looking for. *Hairetikos?* It's hard to recall how long I knelt there, but it was long enough to make my knees ache with gratefulness that I could still walk, even after my truck wreck of the previous spring. Upon leaving, I took a chance on a blessing and dipped my hand in holy water, thinking how my sister once doused her home with the stuff to save a marriage gone bad and their lemon of a car.

When the song ended, the philosopher was talking about Los Alamos, Oppenheimer, and Teller. He was somewhere in the middle of his observation, the beginning of which I seemed to have missed. My grandfather, I wanted to tell him, had played a role in the Manhattan Project, though he had kept it a secret all his life. It wasn't until the old man's funeral that my father revealed it to us: "Now we're all sons of bitches." As the philosopher talked about driving out to see the Trinity site the next morning, I wondered how it must have been for my grandfather to harbor his atomic secret for so long—"I am become Death, the shatterer of worlds." *Can simply being in Albuquerque, "America's Nuclear Weapons Colony," cause excessive radiation exposure? Will the fragments cohere?* I thought about nuclear fission, the Gadget, July 16, 1945, that forty-thousand-foot mushroom cloud, the University of Chicago, Fat Boy, Hiroshima, Nagasaki, the H-bomb (five hundred times stronger than the A-bomb), my grandfather again, Edward Teller's sun lotion and gloves ... I even briefly contemplated driving out in the morning with the philosopher to the Alamogordo Bombing Range until a more pressing question popped into my mind: *Whatever happened to Dennis Hopper in Taos?*

Before I posed my question, the philosopher politely excused himself to head back to the conference for a panel on "Atomic Culture and the Nuclear Age" with particular interest in hearing the paper "'It's the End of the World as We Know It': Nuclear War in Films of the Eighties." Shortly thereafter, Mr. Tecate Man returned with a goofy grin on his face, as if he just received a blow job in the alley behind the cantina (he would have a similar grin, only slightly more contorted, just moments before falling off his barstool the following night). "Our philosopher went back to the hotel," I told him. "I think I've just experienced a red shift."

"You won't believe what I had to go through to get these smokes."

"Let's take a drive down Route 66," I said. "I didn't know you smoked."

"I don't," he returned.

There was no use seeking more answers until we were cruising along Central through downtown Burque. A darkness had settled over the city like a thick serape. Mr. Tecate Man rolled down the windows to snap photos of the neon storefronts and the couples wandering to and from the bars and restaurants. As he shot away, I tried to remember the names of the cheap motels we had passed, a poetry of lodging—Hi Way House, Zia Motor Lodge, the Gaslight Motel, Travel Inn, Imperial Inn, Lorlodge, Stardust Inn, Crossroads, the Aztec advertising "free TV." As we drove, hotels soon outnumbered the people, becoming a lexicon for the travel weary: American Inn, Adobe Manor, Downtown Inn, El Vado Motel, the French Quarter, Grand View, Hacienda, La Mesa, La Puerta, Lazy H, Luna Lodge, Motel 6, Motel 76, Nob Hill Motel, Pioneer, Premier, Relax, Riteway, Roadway, Sand & Sage ... "weekly rentals" and "monthly rentals," "ice," and "air conditioning."

"Who stays in these places?" I asked. "Where do they come from? What are they seeking?"

"Love and clean linen," Mr. Tecate Man replied, "not necessarily in that order." Then he launched into a more sophisticated theory about the survival of such motels and the city's urban development. According to Mr. Tecate Man, these motor lodges catered to curious Europeans seeking the "real" America and to migrant workers needing temporary digs. He suggested city planning had something to do with why these places hadn't yet been bulldozed. His theory involved a flight to the suburban outskirts and city development along the interstate away from inner-urban threats—alcoholic vets, drug-using gangbangers, and illegal aliens (not the type found in Roswell). Perhaps for the first time since his second Dos Equis, he seemed to make perfect sense.

That night, even as we planned on our return up Central to stop at the Frontier diner for late-night tacos or some fried eggs with ham, we drove with our windows down until the strip ended in the desert beyond the valley's sprawl, the ubiquitous glow of its countless street lamps, neon signs, and bright, portentous billboards, long past the red lights of the crowded Pussycat Video Lounge. After Albuquerque it was a long way in any direction to nowhere, to an obelisk in white sand that marked the presence of absence. The rubber tires of our Century glided over the road's rough surface as strong gusts of wind blew us about the old highway. I suggested that we roll up the windows, but Mr. Tecate Man insisted the fresh air would do us good. The farther we drove, the more the desert darkness grew around us. Our headlights, which stretched into the empty distance, hardly seemed to show a way. Farther down the road, a few drops of rain began to splatter across the windshield, then a few more, and still more. When the wind blew hard, a cold mountain rain showered in upon us. Our arms and shirts and the entire inside of the car were quickly soaked. "It's just a rental," Mr. Tecate Man reminded me, so we kept the windows down, letting the fresh air and rain wash over us until only my shoes seemed dry. We were cruising in a good west wind as far as the moment would take us, perhaps to clarity itself. The steadying rain flooded the highway, slowing us some, then disappeared into the sand along the shoulder. Soon there would be a terrific desert blooming—vibrant greens, brilliant yellows, subtle lavenders, pinks, and reds—something that happened briefly only once a year, or sometimes longer. Then I felt it, a sense of knowing welling up within me, alpha and omega, a beginning in this ending or an ending with beginning. "Hope!" I shouted, the sign that points, the thread that binds, "Hope!" In this water music, everything I had come to know. *Shantih. Shantih. Shantih.*

Light & Silence

MEDILOGUE
Introduction to an American Outback

*The Flint Hills make a buckle cinching East to West.
From where I stand ... I can nearly see that stretch of
road where the West begins. The traditional hundredth
meridian be damned; at this latitude the West starts here,
obviously, definitively.*

—William Least Heat-Moon, *PrairyErth*

*South of Emporia the sun ... was sinking over Kansas,
but sinking slowly. For another hour I watched it light the
brown rolling prairies north of Wichita, prairies which the
great trail herds of the nineteenth century had crossed. A
little earlier those plains would have been covered with buffalo, the great southern herd grazing in its millions, with a
mix of nomadic native peoples—Comanche, southern
Cheyenne, Kiowa, Pawnee—following it, living off it. Go
back another ten or twelve thousand years and there would
have been woolly mammoths lumbering around the parts
of the West where the buffalo lumbered later.*

—Larry McMurtry, *Roads:
Driving America's Great Highways*

You're in the middle and I'm on a bridge in Kansas.

You've finally made it to the book's introduction. Don't worry, this is where it belongs, perhaps a metaphor of sorts. It's Midsummer's Eve, the sun is at its greatest distance from the equator, and I'm home in Emporia up high on the Prairie Street highway overpass. Below me on the I-35 interstate, cars and pickups, semis and motor homes pass through town along a concrete river running diagonally across the heartland from Duluth, Minnesota, to Laredo, Texas. I'm up here waiting for the blue moment, that point of transition before sunset somewhere short of dusk, the day's last gasp on this longest day of light in the year. We're in a tornado watch, too, so I'm also checking the skies. Just before the blue moment, weather permitting, the horizon will turn from yellow to orange. Then an iridescent blue will last just long enough to recognize, like silence on the prairie or a pause in the wind that gusts now at a hard clip.

Not much happens in this piece other than some talk about friends and weather; then again, that's everything there is to talk about sometimes. I often tell my freshman writing students—while they read the school newspaper, draw my caricature, fiddle with their belly-button rings, chew gum, eat chips, sip coffee from oversized travel mugs, paint their nails (actually happened), and/or finish homework for their next class—that an introduction is where you explain precisely what it is you're writing about (and avoid ending sentences with prepositions). To those pretending to listen by nodding courteously out of respect or habit, I say it's customary as well to give some sense of direction, to foreshadow links and themes, and if you're really good, provide an intimation of the piece's undercurrents and allusions in a well-organized fashion that employs mellifluous language. For emphasis, I draw on the blackboard a prodigious outline filled with points and subpoints, sometimes even with two colors of chalk; and, if I'm really up to the challenge, I lug our department's Eisenhower-era overhead projector down twenty-two steps from my office to my classroom, pray the bulb works, then fire up examples by former students from the most erudite to inane. Most introductions, I add, should be written and revised after a piece is finished, when you know what it is you've said and have focused the work accordingly. "You're creating a road map for the reader," I emphasize, "a way through the grass!" (the word *grass* raising a few heads, though not in an understanding of the metaphor's significance to our region).

Out of respect for my profession and all of those attentive students I've lectured over the years, I've tried in writing this book's introduction to follow my own advice but ended up here in the middle's Outback on the summer solstice waiting for the blue moment while watching the sky for signs. Maybe I'm seeking connections and cohesion where there is nothing more than the tabula rasa of sky itself, its brilliance or discomforting darkness. Perhaps I've discovered in these essays nothing more than a few brief insights. Like a prospector, maybe all I have is a handful of pyrite, a fool's gold of alarming irony; then again, maybe in small measures, I've located where grace resides, elusive but effulgent.

I'm reminded here of a passage from Thoreau's *Walden* (in my worn copy, I've unintentionally bookmarked my page over the years with a green Care-Free Sugarless Gum wrapper). Free to pursue an experiment in the woods in order "to front only the essential facts of life," Thoreau shows in many moments of brilliance how to see the world about us. In *Walden's* glorious chapter "Spring," a culmination of what he has discussed throughout his sacred book, Thoreau writes how he discovers beauty in what surrounds him, even in a mass of dirt: "Few phenomena gave me more delight than to observe the forms which thawing sand and clay assume in flowing down the sides of a deep cut on the railroad." Time and time again, Thoreau begins with something like sand, its "iron colors, brown, gray, yellowish, and reddish ... running together," then arrives at a moment of brief clarity: "What makes this sand foliage remarkable is its springing into existence thus suddenly." He fills his entire book with such insights and with them shows us how to see better, how to open our eyes to possibility in order to find unexpected harmony and beauty even in the "seemingly conflicting."

Thoreau owes a debt to Emerson, especially his stumbling upon a May-blooming "Rhodera" flourishing with "purplish petals" in the woods that changes how he sees and knows the world. What Emerson and Thoreau discover, I like to call "local knowledge," and what they both appreciate is the surprise of discovery. Yi-Fu Tuan describes the recognition of such knowledge as "topophilia," our "affective ties with the material environment," be they aesthetic, sensory, and/or because of our deep memories. As with Thoreau, Tuan revels in beauty "suddenly revealed," when the environment becomes "the carrier of emotionally charged events or perceived as symbol." What Emerson, Thoreau, Tuan and many other writers, from John Muir to Aldo Leopold, Rachel Carson to Annie Dillard, Edward Abbey to William Least Heat-Moon, develop is a sense of awareness, an appreciation for what occurs in a seemingly chance encounter. Abbey exclaims: "I want to know it all, possess it all, embrace the entire scene intimately, deeply, totally." I like to think my modus operandi is something of a dig—an awareness that can reveal a metaphor, a seeking after the story or myth that structures our vision or helps explain it, a love for the comedy of the incongruous, irony that vanishes with epiphany.

This evening, my feet dangling from the overpass, I feel as if I'm high in a crow's nest on a tall ship. To the east, where the sky is darkening, the land flattens in a typically Kansas fashion all the way to Kansas City, 120 miles away. To the west, tall highway signs at Industrial Road Exit 128 glow in the dying light. Most of these places, except the McDonald's and the Golden Corral, weren't here three years ago. Perhaps somebody in big business on a cross-country drive during a midlife crisis figured out it's a long way on a dark night from nowhere to a somewhere familiar to suburbanites. Many consider such corporate colonization to be a sign of prosperity in a community like ours that owes its allegiance to American beef—Candlewood Suites (new), Fairfield (new), Holiday Inn Express (new), Applebees (two years old), Village Inn (two years old, and most people are still waiting for their order), Prairie Port (new truck stop), Wendy's (attached to new truck stop), Staples (two years old), Super Wal-Mart (renovated last summer).

Toward Wichita, 100 miles southwest, the highway becomes a tollway through the Flint Hills grasslands. Of any book I know on the Kansas tallgrass prairie, nothing compares with the eloquence and depth of William Least Heat-Moon's *PrairyErth*, a masterpiece of Melvillean proportions and enough of a vocabulary-raiser to give any writer an anxiety of influence, but a must-read nonetheless. "The prairie," Heat-Moon writes, "is not a topography that shows its all but rather a vastly exposed place of concealment, like the geodes so abundant in the county [Chase County], where the splendid lies within the plain cover." The I-35 tollway underneath me passes through this prairie expanse, a favorite drive of Larry McMurtry, with some of the most spectacular, uninterrupted, and unspoiled views of tallgrass prairie anywhere in the world. One night in late March during range-burning season, I drove the highway home from Wichita to find the hills glowing with fire lines and pastures blazing a brilliant orange. Winds calm, the smell of smoke hung everywhere in the air like a temple's incense. It would be un-American if the state didn't charge a $3.00 fee (3¢ per mile) for passage along such a road. At night, they ought to charge more, because the sky is so dark out there, it can feel as if you're driving through space. When I do drive in the evening, I tend to lose myself in so much sky, the glitter of a million suns. I've been known in good weather to pull off the road at a cattle pens exit (they really exist) just to stretch myself back over the car's warm hood and watch the sky for a bit. On a map measuring light pollution in America, we're one of the few places left where the sky at night still looks like the sky should look, and has looked for thousands and thousands of years. On such nights, you can almost feel a part of that deep time, as if something, somewhere inside, perhaps the stardust of your bones, still hums with the remote frequencies from where it came.

If the approaching storm doesn't get here first, I will watch the sun eventually set on this longest of days. Way up north in Nuuk, where for half the year the sun hardly shines at all, Greenlanders celebrate this long-lasting light, their season of bright fire, as a holiday. If I'm not first blown off this bridge, I will celebrate, more simply, a brief resplendence of blue. Wherever the drivers beneath me may be going, they better hurry. Moisture up from the Texas Gulf gives the air a sticky feel, heavy and explosive. At any moment swirling winds with thunder and lightning, hail, and rain, might come tumbling over the western horizon. Flash-flood weather, it's the kind we get most often in the late spring's tornado season. This year only a few towns have been flattened by cyclones, but flattened nonetheless. Along the highway, everybody sails by in a hurry against a hard chop, some perhaps to beat the front, probably more just to get through Kansas. If they're like me, keeping an eye out for severe weather, they're listening to the tollway's AM 1610 broadcast with its tin-sounding recorded voice that crackles like rain.

The longer I'm up here, the harder the wind begins to blow. Quite frankly, I'm worried. Weather like this I know. Years ago in 1980, I was in Lawrence, Kansas, about a month after an F2 (winds of 113 to 157 miles per hour) ripped through town at 4:35 p.m. on the last day of May, peak tornado season. That night in Lawrence, the memory of the F2 still fresh in everybody's minds, I was standing on a porch of a once-dilapidated but now restored turn-of-the-century rambler on Mississippi Street watching another severe storm pass through town. I remember the heavy air, like the air tonight, the brilliant lightning in the distance, but mostly the terrific thunder so loud the unstable porch shook as if in an earthquake. I was a fearless fourteen, soon to be a high-school freshman—what was a little rain and thunder, a few swirling clouds, the possibility of another F2? It would be years before I discovered that Lawrence was the boyhood home of Langston Hughes, who hated the Free State's racism, or that the vodka-swizzling William Burroughs lived only a few streets over with his guns, cat, and visitors like Allen Ginsberg.

Given what I knew could happen when the storm came, I should have felt more fear. After being hit by a Cadillac when I was twelve, I developed an overwhelming sense of my mortality, enough to set aside before bed one minute (no more, no less) to pray that I would live another day and, if I didn't, that my soul would be saved from eternal damnation. I understood the unpredictable nature of most events, how difficult it is to forecast the haphazard direction a tornado will go. Perhaps a storm's rage is something of a metaphor, a sign to be read, the genesis of a logic that sets me searching and desiring to make sense of things that lend themselves, or not, to knowing—those dammed fragments, as Pound and Eliot would have lamented. Of course, none of my early teenage angst had anything to do with the fact that my junior high's biology teacher was a serial killer, nor that one summer I rode shotgun in his Bronco, where under my seat he kept the chains and rope used to strangle hitchhiking boys.

That evening in Lawrence, I smoked what I imagined might actually be my last Marlboro, though it was really the beginning of a filthy habit that would take me years to break. As the wind swirled madly about me signaling what could be the end of the world as I knew it, I stood my ground. When the F2 blew through town, it had rolled over the local K-Mart and everything else in its path, strewing debris everywhere, turning trailers into kindling, tossing cars about as if hurled by the very hands of Hercules. Chancy weather.

At any moment the skies on this longest day of light could turn violent. I can't deny we need the rain here in Emporia,

"Front Porch to the Flint Hills" (though few people actually have or sit on porches). This spring, the early heat has already stunted the tall grass, though last year the grasses grew so high you could barely see a bison grazing in the distance. "Seven years of fat, then seven years of lean," my friend Amy has predicted. "We're headed toward lean." She knows. Amy lives in the country just outside of town in an old white farmhouse that creaks in stormy weather like a tall-mast ship. "It's like traveling the high seas with Captain Ahab," she says, then all I can think about is Amy in a scene resembling Dorothy's in *The Wizard* when her house spins about in the funnel cloud—Dorothy come undone—just before everything turns Technicolor and the Munchkins start singing. Allusions to *The Wizard* in Kansas are much more than worn-out cultural references, they're our cultural heritage here, against which we must constantly measure ourselves.

The stuff of legend, weather is serious business. Emporia, like communities throughout the state, regularly tests its severe weather sirens, and local TV touts its live Doppler radar ready to zoom in to street level just moments before a tornado churns everything into useless junk. Many Kansans, especially those in Topeka where an F5 (261 to 318 miles per hour) hit on June 8, 1966, killing 16 and injuring 450, can still repeat a famous warning by then-WIBW TV anchorman, Bill Curtis, "For God's sake, take cover!" One of the worst tornadoes in Kansas history, another F5, blew away the town of Udall, southeast of Wichita, on May 25, 1955, killing some 75 people. Prior to Udall, the record death count from a single tornado stood at 66 for the Irving tornado on May 30, 1879. In the mere forty-year span from 1887 to 1927 there were approximately 72 deaths statewide, not counting deaths from more minor tornadoes. The largest single death and injury count in recent years, 19 dead and 243 injured, goes to an outbreak of tornadic activity (ranging from F1 to F5) in an around the Wichita–El Dorado corridor. Late May and June are the worst months of the year for cyclones, though they can happen at any time anywhere. Some in Emporia like to repeat an old folk notion that *a tornado won't hit near a river*, especially a town like Emporia located between two rivers, the Neosho to our north and the Cottonwood to our south. However, 6 people died here on June 8, 1974, in an F4 (207 to 260 miles per hour) injuring some 177 people. These people will tell you never to trust the following weather predictors:

Expect rain and maybe severe weather when dogs eat grass.

If a dog pulls his feet up high while walking, a change in the weather is coming.

When you look out your window to find your dogs jumping around and ducking, it's a sign that it's hailing.

One of the orthopedists my wife works for has told us about his being in the old A&P's checkout line with his daughter at 6:00 p.m. when the '74 twister hit. They were waiting to buy 7-Up and Uncle Ben's Brown Rice when the lights began to flicker and the roof began to bounce, seconds before they dove for cover against the checkout stand. As the twister passed over them, the windows blew out, and they lost their brand new car to a metal sign from what was then an auto parts store across the street. Their sedan destroyed, they had to walk home, where along the way a neighbor spotted them, then drove the good doctor to the hospital to begin triage with the many injured. Even with two rivers and the predictions of jumping dogs, in the last fifty years there have been some 35 tornadoes in our county alone.

About the beginning of March each year, the State tries to get out the word that everybody should have a plan. I'm partial to a passage I found on creating a "Family Disaster Supply Kit," a list that seems to apply largely to saving families with money. In addition to crowbar, latex gloves, and MREs (Meals Ready to Eat), the list suggests securing the following: copies of stocks and bonds, wills, insurance policies, contracts, and deeds; copies of passports, social security cards, and immunization records; records of credit card account numbers, bank account numbers, and family records (birth, marriage, death certificates); and an inventory of valuable household goods with a list of important telephone numbers. It adds a courteous reminder to "help injured or trapped persons," which I assume is what you do when not worrying about a big financial loss or leaving the country. Nonetheless, I find curiously missing from the list a Bible and water, both of which for many Kansans would be more important than a crowbar and copies of stocks and bonds.

On a night like tonight, I might need such a kit. Boy Scout that I am, I have prepared an evacuation plan for my family. Because we really have no money, I have disregarded most of the above suggestions, though I did seriously consider the latex gloves. My plan goes like this: if we have time for anything but a profound "I love you" before being blown away, my wife grabs the flashlight, the baby, the radio, and diaper bag (in that order), and I run around in the dark trying to gather our cats into two bulky plastic carriers (we must bring two because our Siamese tend to spit and strike at each other when confined together in emergency situations; the carriers are also critical because in them I have stored spare disks of my writing oeuvre for them to piss on when they become stressed). The next step is for us to descend together to the first floor from our third-floor apartment, which, resembling an aquarium, has large, sliding glass windows on two sides. In the middle of the hallway just below street level, we imagine we'll stand a better chance of living. Since our building was actually grazed by the '74 tornado, I also have to have some faith in probability theory, which would suggest a greater chance for our survival in subsequent tornadic events. Part of the plan also includes that the both of us wear bicycle helmets for further protection, but my wife refuses to comply, even more so after a previous evacuation when my helmet received much ridicule from our neighbors (while I understand my fashion blunder, I will, of course, be the last laughing in the event that flying debris slices through their thick heads).

Tonight, before heading out to the overpass, I recommended to my eighty-five-year-old neighbor, who lives below me, that she prepare for the possibility of an evacuation. "The brick is solid," she said with such conviction that I didn't have the heart to tell her how the bricks holding up my balcony were crumbling. She also prefers not to be wakened when the sirens blow. If you've lived that long and have seen the building already hit once, I suppose there's no reason to fear tornadoes.

The last time the alarms sounded nothing went as planned. Instead of staying on the first floor with my wife and baby after a successful evacuation, I ran back upstairs to wake up all the old ladies who didn't show up in the hallway. My bicycle helmet strapped tightly to my head, I pounded every door on the second floor where these widows live, two with hearing aids and another who has trouble walking. As the wind thrashed hail and rain against the hall's large, south-facing windows, I questioned if I'd make it back safely downstairs to join my wife and baby girl huddled with our caged cats and a diaper bag containing Pampers and a bottle of Similac.

Running up and down the hallway, I hadn't felt such fear in years, a fear I didn't much feel at fourteen that night in Lawrence when I hadn't done much living, come to appreciate expensive wine, or had much to lose. Perhaps the last time I felt a similar fear was when my wife and I lost a hiking trail near sunset when coming down a mountain in California's Anza Borrego desert. While she teared up with wails of "We're lost! We're lost!" I faked a confident knowledge of how we had only to rappel down a twenty-foot cliff to join up with the trail. In the end, only our camera suffered permanent physical damage after I threw our packs over the ledge moments before we foolishly hung from the cliff top in order to lessen the distance of our drops—such is the elasticity of youth. The cliché is true: I never felt more alive than when contemplating that fall. Years later on the night of our truck rollover, an evening that must have given pause even to the angels who found us in the crushed, upside-down vehicle, my wife just days from giving birth, I didn't have enough time to feel much of anything until we entered our apartment later that night after returning from the hospital, our cats waiting at the door for us as they usually do. At that moment, looking at those cats, I felt that I'd walked into a new life, that although the scenery was the same, along with our cats' routine, I wasn't, and that what happened and how it turned out was largely an inexplicable, random event. I somehow felt marked, too, that wherever I went I had the word *survivor* tattooed on my forehead. I had entered a vortex and somehow came out the other side with a permanently bad back and glass shards in my hands, but still alive with my wife and soon-to-be-born baby. Not a day goes by when I don't think of that night as a lucky roll of the dice in the ultimate game of craps. While I'm only a La-Z-Boy psychologist at best, perhaps all of this has something to do with why, whenever I can, I like to sit on the edge of this bridge high above the highway to welcome the blue moment.

Such thoughts remind me of a friend of mine, may he rest in peace, who learned to fly a small Cessna shortly after retiring. As he told me himself, he woke up one May morning and decided to become a pilot. A year before he took his first flying lesson, his wife passed away from breast cancer; not long after he buried her, his best friend's wife died of leukemia; then another friend divorced after twenty-something years of marriage and a handful of kids. "Flying felt right," he told me.

With part of his retirement savings, Frank bought a 1946 Cessna 140, a small silver plane with a single red propeller, like something you might be able to build in your basement. He took lessons, bought himself a blue flight suit with his name embroidered over his heart. After he passed his licensing test, I gave him a red scarf. "Keep it out of the propeller," I told him. "If I die from choking, you can put it in that book of yours." "Who could have predicted you'd become a pilot?" "Then write me into a baker. I've always wanted to be a baker." Because he was old and cranky, I could let him say such things with impunity.

"The scarf will make you fly better, but not necessarily look better," I told him. On a good day in a pale light, he didn't seem as rough as elm bark with hair white as cottonwood seed. The flight suit did well to hide his gut; he'd been in better shape when his wife did the cooking, was lucky he still had his own teeth.

Just as he learned to read the signs in books, Frank learned to read all those dials and gauges in his cockpit. The way he told it, in order to be sure up wasn't down or down wasn't up, the key to navigation was learning to trust the instruments over what he believed to be true in front of him. I can picture how it must have been for Frank up there buzzing through a cloud, see him checking his altimeter, then practicing rolls until he could no longer tell which way was a flight to the moon or a dive earthwards. Part of not crashing, or maybe just living, meant giving up what we think seems right.

I like to imagine I can see Frank passing overhead, the flippity-flop-flop-flop flippity-flop-flop-flop of his propeller, his plane coming out of the clouds. High over the town, he could see a quilt of small farms scattered in the bottomlands, the crooked runs of our muddy rivers, the distant Flint Hills, that uninterrupted expanse of some of the last remaining tallgrass prairie on the planet. As a crow flies, he could be in Denver in a few hours, dine in Dallas, or follow the Missouri to its confluence with the Mississippi. I imagine him buzzing my bridge, coming in low enough to give me a good scare. I know he'd be smiling, and it makes me glad that in flying he found a way to do it again, even if he didn't live very long afterward.

Perhaps to survive in the out here, you need to cultivate a way of seeing all your own. Award-winning photographer Larry Schwarm, who graciously provided the photograph of prairie fire, *Fire Lines, Chase County, Kansas*, for the cover of my first book, is one such visionary. Son of a dirt farmer, he's a lanky, middle-aged, native Kansan with a rough beard of salt and pepper. His cheeks seem as etched as the Cottonwood's riverbanks in August, his eyes covered by round spectacles, squinty as if from looking through too many viewfinders. He exudes "cool" as only somebody truly cool could know. Every once in a while he puts on a tie and we all look surprised. Before fires, Larry used to shoot food for the print media in Milwaukee, the kind of pictures that leave you sweaty for an enchilada.

Larry does his fire work in early spring, mid-March to mid-April, during range-burning season when ranchers set fire to the prairie to cultivate new growth. In town, a thin white ash collects on almost everything and the smell of fire hangs in the air. Before ranchers began to set fire to the fields, the Indians here did the same to create better forage for game and to draw back the buffalo to the rich new grass. Before them, lightning from the Pawnee's Tirawa created prairie fire in a time before the marking of time. William Least Heat-Moon points out how fire has shaped the prairie for some 25 million years, "The four horsemen of the prairie are tornado, locust, drought, and fire, and the greatest of these is fire, a rider with two faces because for everything taken it makes a return in equal measure." Signs along the highway—RANGE BURNING AREA. DO NOT DRIVE INTO DENSE SMOKE—warn novice motorists to pull to the right shoulder to stop driving if they can't see the highway.

For most of this brief season, Larry spends much of his time driving about the Flint Hills in his maroon Volvo looking for burning fields. Typically, he goes in the late afternoon to shoot at twilight, what for a photographer must be some of the trickiest but most satisfying light of the day. I've often wanted to ask Larry to take me along, but I understand how a genius like him needs to go at it alone, not be bothered by the banter of a loquacious writer. So I have to imagine it all, the way writers do their work even when the facts present themselves. In the Flint Hills backcountry, if his radio had not really died many years ago, maybe Larry would be listening to our local 97 Country, because maybe like me he knows how lonely back roads make the best places to listen to country. Or maybe he'd be listening to Gershwin on NPR—he's the kind of guy who would. But perhaps he'd listen for the weather, because in spring, everybody around here listens to the weather—lives depend on it.

I imagine, to sniff out a fire, Larry drives with his windows down, his camera on the seat beside him, a nicked-up tripod bouncing on the back seat along with some old beer cans that haven't yet jumped out into a ditch. His Volvo, an odd choice, I've always thought, for a motorist who drives the back roads of Kansas, moves at a good clip, groaning over the gravel, spitting dust and rocks that clunk against the muffler or ping off his tailpipe. Maybe Larry, because he knows it'll be a long night, washes down a sandwich with some trucker coffee, that highly caffeinated kind from quick shops like Casey's General Store, or perhaps he just takes a good swig from the gallon of water he always keeps handy for thirst or flame. Smudged with ash and smelling like smoke, he'll shoot a fire until all that's left are blackened fields, some still smoldering, strewn with limestone and flint rock. Sometimes he gets so close to a raging blaze he singes his shoes, even the hair on his arms. He used to wear high-topped boots to keep his ankles from getting burned, but after once having been trapped by a fire and needing to run hard for a long stretch to get away, he makes sure to wear shoes good enough for sprinting. On the advice of a seasoned rancher, Larry always carries a pack of matches, too. If something were to happen, if he broke an ankle or snake got him, he could light a small fire, then move into the burned area to escape an approaching blaze, much as the pioneers themselves set firebreaks around their homes.

I know from Larry's work and from talking with him in the off season—he's got no time for questions from annoying writers in March—that he seeks not just fire but color and perspective, something elemental, a Rothko of flames. In his pictures, now collected in his prize-winning book *On Fire / Larry Schwarm*, I've seen fearsome blazes from thick, dry thatch shooting higher than steel windmills. "Hell of Fires!" George Catlin would have called it, something like the towering flames and suffocating smoke of his own *Prairie Meadows Burning* or the suicidal image of *Bison and Prairie Fire*. But Larry can find fire's gentle side, too, capturing a field's slow burn, sinuous fire lines glowing in shades of yellow and orange on a dark night.

From my bridge, I can sometimes count three or more fires burning at once in the fields circling town, as if the entire earth will eventually go up in flames the very way it came blasting into being. Of anybody I know, Larry seems the closest to understanding these seasons, this land and its hills of tallgrass. His work reveals something mythical, something deep within us, that mystery of origins in the forge of creation. When I see these fires and find the ash, I consider it a blessing of sorts, the way each spring Catholic priests rub the ash of last year's sacred palm onto the foreheads of their parishioners to mark the start of the Lenten season: "for dust thou art, and unto dust shalt thou return" (Genesis 3:19). The bright bonfires celebrating St. John's Day on Midsummer's Eve seem right, too, fire itself perhaps the oldest of ritual symbols. Out here, this scattering of ash in the wind is a way to believe in the sanctity of spring, how soon, with rain returning, grasses will rise up from the charred earth.

Tornado watch or not, I like it up here, the feel of the moist air against my skin, these winds of danger. It's possible to believe that the entire world passes under me, everybody going somewhere, everything moving except me twenty feet above the commotion. I'm on an edge as close to the sky as you can get around here with only a rusty guardrail to save me from flying off with the geese.

While I wait for the blue moment, I like to count the vehicles going east and west, the seconds between them, the numbers of cars versus trucks, or the total number that pass in an hour. Sometimes, for variety, I only count semis or shit-splattered cattle trailers, maybe just Ford Rangers or Toyota Corollas, domestics or foreigns. Typically late in the day, fifty-two seconds seems to be the longest interval without traffic east or west. In the winter months on a wind-whipped day after a passing front, when ice and snow cover the roadway like a thermal blanket, it's possible that I might not see a vehicle in either direction for an astounding four or five entire minutes (every few years KDOT actually closes down the highway, but only in extreme blizzard conditions). When a lone truck finally passes, its roof piled with drifts, icicles dripping from its frame, snow blows in all directions like a herd of wild broncos passing through town. When the snow finally settles, that's when I begin counting the minutes again. Last year, I once hit the seven-minute mark, my all-time record, which, to anybody who has ever watched highway traffic, is a long, long time to feel so alone along an interstate. But something always passes.

Often I muse about the lives in the traffic under me—truckers and troubadours, wives and lovers, divorcées and retirees, felons and perverts, priests and pimps—and imagine where they are going—cocaine runners from Laredo making a delivery to dealers in Minneapolis; a Navy squid coming home to a prairie sea; migrant workers from El Salvador en route to jobs at the IBP slaughterhouse; a trucker from Des Moines carrying hides to the tannery in St. Joe, Missouri; a losing football team in a yellow bus on what seems the longest ride of their lives; a church group in a van that seeks to save souls in Dodge City. Together we are witnesses to a common moment, a chance convergence, something like matter colliding in space.

When I'm not watching traffic, I sometimes dig through the grass and bushes at the side of the bridge to see what I can find, but I have to be careful. In the heartland, there exists an unspoken tyranny of the majority, where almost anything out of the ordinary is suspect. In other words, you don't want too many people to know how you see or what you do, so as not to appear to set yourself too far apart from the community and end up with nobody to talk to in the Food 4 Less checkout line. Nevertheless, from trash diving at our local recycle center and other places about town, I've come to conclude that trash, or that which gets discarded, reveals more about our community than almost anything else: just consult Wallace Stevens or any archaeologist, archaeology being in part the study of cultural trash.

Garbage currently in the bushes and weeds along the Prairie Street overpass: 17 cigarette butts (counted in only one square foot), 4 cans of Coors, 1 can of Coors Light, 2 cans of Bud Light, 1 can of Keystone Light, 4 bottles of Miller Lite, 1 bottle of Amaretto (generic), 1 bottle of Jägermeister ("hunt master," made from 56 herbs and spices rivaling in mystery only Colonel Sanders's secret spice blend), 2 cans of Diet Coke, 1 can of Diet Dr Pepper, 1 can of Diet Pepsi, 1 plastic bottle of Diet Pepsi (12 oz.), 3 blue plastic Wal-Mart bags, 4 Diamond Card lotto scratchers (losers), 3 $50 Fever lotto scratchers (losers), 4 Big Fat Wallet lotto scratchers (losers), 2 Kansas Speedway lotto scratchers (losers), 3 Double Doubler lotto scratchers (losers), 2 Triple Tripler lotto scratchers (losers), 1 Wrigley's Extra Spearmint Gum wrapper, 1 Marlboro Lights (box), 3 Topps baseball cards (Bret Boone, Magglio Ordonez, Mike Lansing), 2 car keys, and 3 torn-out pages from the *Over 40* porn mag picturing Jo Jo Love, 2000 Model of the Year Contest Winner (actual quote from page: "I always get a kick out of exposing myself ... the average range of my fans is between 24 and 36").

Another friend of mine who recently moved out of town has a similar affection for odd hobbies, his being the tracking of trains and their graffiti at the Burlington Northern Santa Fe (BNSF) rail yard (and eluding the railroad cops). Perhaps it was simply fate that brought us together or maybe it was something more divine. With his mountain bike and a notebook, Scott scouted the yard, then recorded engine numbers and graffiti on boxcars, typically left by urban gangs from Chicago to Los Angeles. Scott sees graffiti as a form of public poetry on a moving sign-board, a text, sometimes readable and sometimes not, that he finds beautiful for its random juxtapositions—"I Love You Camilla," "Chrome Felons 97," "Coyote Cojo," "Eat More Pussy." Scott also tracks graffiti scrawled under highway over-passes and says he owes one of his best finds to a state trooper friend, who took him out one day, I assume when off duty, to the Thorndale underpass not far from town. Perhaps because of my past sitting under an Edens Expressway overpass in suburban Chicago's Wilmette to smoke cigarettes or share a joint between classes at Loyola Academy, I'm partial to underpass graffiti; some that I created is probably still in existence.

I think Scott's found poems and the graffiti that shapes them express as much truth as almost any other art. Whether it's a pre-Columbian petroglyph or a slogan from a teen with a spray can, both come from artists seeking to make sense of their places, to re-present the world. They seek in signs, as do writers with their poems, to bring greater clarity; and, as with poetry, graffiti is emotionally charged—"Kansas Is No California Mutha Fuckas." There can be found in such raw lines—"I have a big goat billy and he sucks big goat testicles like yours"—the urgency of a moment, something that must be said, crude lan-guage that subverts polite speech and contests social boundaries in its self-assertion. Such work is not unlike Jean-Michel Basquiat's aestheticized graffiti in works such as *Untitled (Quality)*, 1983, that maps and critiques history; *Worthy Constituents* that reveres Black music; the marvelous abstractions of *Untitled* (1981) with its crucifixion allusions; or, one of my personal favorites for its postcolonial criticism, *Native Carrying Some Guns, Bibles, Amorites on Safari, 1982.*

Prior to coming to Emporia for graduate study in English, where he developed an interest in the found poem, Scott had been a minister in Missouri. "Sermons," he said when I first found out he was a former man of the cloth who drove a red Camaro, "I have enough for an entire year of Sundays." When I'm up in my overpass perch above the traffic, I often think of Scott. He would probably be amazed by that fact. When I first met him, I was with a first-semester writing class in our small university library, the William Allen White library, named, as with many places in town, after the Pulitzer Prize–winning journalist, Emporia's biggest claim to fame besides boxed beef.

The day of my initial encounter with Scott, he was all spiffed up with large wire-framed glasses and a blue polyester suit with matching tie. His white shirt seemed starched enough to stand up through an entire sermon. Before he confessed to me, months later, his formal religious training, I had him pegged as a minister, or, if you will, a Bible-pounder of sorts. It's not unusual on our campus, located on the Bible Belt's buckle, for preachers to come to drum up a crusade. Artists of the oratory, they give good old-fashioned stump speeches, complete with much gesticulation, intrusive pointing, and the frequent use of words such as Jezebel to verbally attack possibly wayward coeds with the goal of shaming them into faithful submission.

Kansas has a tradition of people on such missions, typified by the likes of abolitionist John Brown (a true visionary) and teetotaler Carrie Nation. Here's a portion of the song "In Kansas" that perhaps Nation and missionaries like her enjoyed for its mocking moral warrants:

Oh, they say that drink's a sin in Kansas
They say that drink's a sin in Kansas
They say that drink's a sin

So they guzzle all they kin,
Then they throw it up again.

The *Tales Out of School* newsletter from the Center for Great Plains Studies at Emporia State University suggests to elementary school teachers that singing and talking about this song would make for a good classroom activity and advises telling students that "It's a song made up by ordinary people, like us"—now that's a fetching irony. Though I am uncertain of my own ordinariness, I am partial to the song's additional verses concerning how Kansans "chaw tobacco thin ... And they spit it on their chin. And they lap it up again," not to mention Kansans who grow small potatoes and "eat them hides and all." It's a wonder the song ends inviting "Come, all who want to roam to Kansas ... And be happy with your doom in Kansas." Nevertheless, perhaps what drives crusaders such as Nation in their visions of doom comes from the ennui of isolation, or maybe it's a radical frontier spirit, the individualism of "Puritanism transplanted" as Carl L. Becker has noted, bent on engendering conformity and homogeneity, the ingredients of ordinariness, come hell or high water.

That day in the library, I imagine Scott might have taken me as someone who needed saving before he approached to ask a few questions about the college in a distinguishable Arkansas drawl. All that time he asked about our program, I wasn't sure if he was putting me on or if his innocent questions were a prelude to giving me some literature about sin. Because of the prevalence of soul savers in our town, I've developed a good collection of pamphlets from visiting preachers and their missionary faithful who have showed up on campus or at my front door:

"The Battle of Your Soul: Saved or Lost"
"Entertainment, Amusements, Fun: What Does God Say?"
"The Sin of Immorality: Purity, Love, Happy Homes, Confidence, Lust, Shame, Fear, Broken Homes, Loneliness"

"Your Life Is Going on Record" (a personal favorite)
"Repentance: A Godly Sorrow for Sin"
"The Answer to Your Problems" (one I'd send to every member of my family if they wouldn't become personally offended)
And, of course, "What Must I Do To Be Saved?"

When Scott got around to asking for my name, initially I considered it to be quite unfortunate, something similar to the large billboard just outside of town along the highway that welcomes visitors with ACCEPT JESUS CHRIST AND YOU SHALL BE SAVED—OR REGRET IT FOREVER. I certainly didn't want to get any more evangelical pamphlets, or worse, welcome an apartment visitation later that evening—sometimes these types can be aggressive, especially at front doors, as they inquire about personal behavior using words like "masturbation" that I know can be heard all the way down the hall. Then again, first impressions can be misleading.

To make a long story short, I'm glad I had the opportunity to know Scott before he graduated and took a job teaching composition at Barton County Community College in Great Bend, Kansas. He showed me another way to see, a way to find meaning in the fragments. Of all of his discoveries on the sides of trains, I'm partial to his finding of the adjacent red spray paintings of "Fuck" and "Jesus Saves" on a Santa Fe boxcar that must have made innumerable trips across our nation. Scott's found poetry from rail yards is the stuff of genius for how it captures the essential truth of place, as with these lines from a piece of his called "Midnight Mischief" that trump any sunflower poems of Ginsberg with their raw energy and intrinsic railway rhythms.

Part 2=Cattle Cars in Yellow

Fuck You—Fuck DC—Blow Me Bitch—Frag

Moxican Movement—Pero Puto—Loball—EYL
Kill smokin 65 ace 68—VKS and DVS, Rollin 60's
Bitch you know the side world motherfuckin ride

Perhaps we should all look for signs on trains, in burning
fields, in the desert, while eating burritos, or in the sky—
"Surrender Dorothy!"

When I look at the highway rolling off as it does into the now-
red horizon, I often feel the need to get away west of town for a
few days. Somehow in going off for a time, feeding that wester-
ing of my blood, I come to know myself better. Perhaps my wan-
derlust resembles something coded in the migrating geese who
often fly over this bridge. Sometimes they fly alone, other times
in inseparable pairs; most often they fly together in a formation
that dips and rises, a few pushing ahead as some from behind try
to catch up. They nest for a season, move on somewhere else,
then return, perhaps drawn back by an innate homing on invisible magnetic lines. Maybe these birds and my pilot friend know
that the best perspective west from the Outback can be found
up there where, if any pattern exists, it can be seen more clearly. Perhaps up in the sky's silence with only a plane's motor
humming its prayers, something elusive might manifest itself,
not something otherworldly but something out there all along,
if only we are listening for it. Maybe, too, there are patterns to
be discovered in lines of fire burning across a field, in what's left
behind in the ashes or what rises up from them. We can, as
Edward Abbey suggests, "learn to perceive in water, leaves, and
silence more than sufficient of the absolute and marvelous."
*This earth, these muddy rivers, this wind, these doves, these coyotes
in the hills, these lolling dogwoods, these crows and singing frogs, this
prairie, this poem, these stars tonight about to shine—*
In this short span of time on Midsummer's Eve, I've gone on
far too long for an introduction. I apologize to those who dozed

off in the Cessna section, who desire a succinct summary or a recap at this point. I'm not even sure I can make all the pieces fit in a conventional sense, but at least I'm sure that that's not my point. Somehow in this verbal vortex, like the wind now swirling around me, I like to believe that all this circling and layering has served as a proper model and introduction, a weaving through the Outback's tallgrass so to say—part metaphor, part thing itself. Fireflies have just begun to flit about in the ditches on both sides of the highway, cars and trucks are flipping on their headlights. I have no more time for explanations. The next few moments will be everything I'm after, a brief but spectacularly resonant glow of resplendent blue. Jubla! Jubla! Rejoice in this evanescent luminescence, this last light on this longest day of light in the year. *Reveal the wizard*, the west wind whispers, *if you can.*

Icons, Myths & Amusements

CURIOUS ABRUPT QUESTIONINGS
The Lure of Glitz and Glam

The impalpable sustenance of me from all things at all hours
   of the day,
The simple, compact, well-join'd scheme, myself disintegrated
   every one disintegrated yet part of the scheme, ...

What is it then between us?

—Walt Whitman, "Crossing Brooklyn Ferry"

One can look at Las Vegas from a mile away on Route 91
and see no buildings, no trees, only signs. But such signs!

—Tom Wolfe, "Las Vegas (What?) Las Vegas
(Can't hear you! Too noisy) Las Vegas!!!!"

"Heartattack, heartattack, heartattack, heart attack,
heartATTACK, heart-ATTACK, HEART ATTACK, HEART-A-
TACK!" I tell the cowboy next to me in the black Stetson and
string tie. "Craps action, man. Know what I'm saying?"
Although the Tom Wolfe literary parody is lost on him, he gets
what I mean, has dollar signs in his eyes, can see the chips
splashed across the table, the stickman ready, the bounce of
those bones in a fleeting moment of chance, the come or don't

come peppered with cries of agony or ecstasy before the roll settles that perhaps reveal more about the nature of our existence than anything I know. "The only other time in my life I ever heard the word 'come' shouted," I say to him, "was from this gal I once slept with in college who prefaced with 'don't' and followed with 'in me' throughout her orgasm." He's not sure whether to laugh or get up, and even I know that was a bit over the top, somewhat too brazen for casual conversation, too Hunter Thompson. Surely, the bravado necessary in any exchange about Las Vegas must be forgiven. But he's no priest and I can tell he's ready now to end our conversation. So in silence, we wait together, including our pilot with the stars-and-stripes tie, for the next plane out of DFW's Gate 57 to Las Vegas.

The check-in line now winds down the terminal, as if for a ride on a roller coaster at Six Flags. Nothing seems to be happening too swiftly. My fellow travelers on this holiday weekend in July seem relaxed, the calm before the neon storm. Women parade about in sundresses with spaghetti-thin straps, husbands sport khaki Dockers with pastel Polo tops, children in T-shirts advertise for Disney. For this brief moment before our trip begins, we share in our anticipation something special together—lights, whistles, cheap prime rib, the songs of sirens. We can't wait for our first pull of the one-armed bandit, our first throw of the red dice, a double-down if opportunity presents herself (something that sounds suspiciously like a Jacuzzi come-on). There's no place on the planet that compares; it's perhaps the most notable stretch of desert after the Egyptian pyramids— and there's even a pyramid there now—"Only in America!" boxing promoter Don King would say. We're off to Fantasy Island, or as my father called it on his yearly pilgrimage, Disneyland for adults, but now parents bring their children. It's been called other things over time—Sin City, Paradise Valley, City of Broken Dreams, and my personal favorite, Lost Wages.

Such trips need to begin somewhere, some place. When going to Vegas, there's no place like the airport, in the moments before anticipation becomes satiated, to collect yourself, to make promises you'll never keep. To truly know who we are, we need to look at what we love and ask why. As the author Michael Ventura has put it, Vegas is a city with "the odds on anything." I'm willing to bet most folks waiting in line are return-trippers like me, people who don't get enough satisfaction on a three-night stay so they keep going back for more. Some even retire there to whittle away their health and retirement savings in front of the hypnotizing slots, where it's possible, when caught up so completely in the myth of El Dorado, to lose all sense of the self, the aching knees, sore back, that troubling incontinence of old age.

We returners are the survivors—some lucky, some not—we already know about the perpetual $1.99 steak and egg breakfast, which used to be a buck. We know about the complete prime rib dinner for $5.99, the white tigers at the Mirage, Siegfried and Roy's love affair, the pirate show at Treasure Island, the simulated New York, even the circus acts performed nightly on stage and in many hotel rooms up and down the Strip. Before all this, Frank, Sammy, Liza, Redd Foxx, Elvis, and Wayne Newton caught the fever, boom and bust. Where the sun bleaches everything, nothing lasts long. To think that Nevada had once been a humid land dotted with lakes seems almost impossible on a dry, windy summer day in the low hundreds. A better name for a town that continues to re-invent itself might have been Phoenix, but that was already taken.

Our plane is an hour late, not unusual by DFW standards. In fact, I've never taken a plane in or out of Dallas that was on time. For tardiness, DFW ranks up there with LAX, ORD, JFK, and ATL. DFW could well be the slowest, most inefficient airport on earth, perhaps the entire universe. It's an unfortunate irony that DFW's major carrier calls itself American. The airport acronym might just as well stand for "Do Finish Waiting."

I've waited so many minutes in the crowded terminals of DFW that I've come to feel sentimental about it. Perhaps the airport merchants have a hand in such delays, an implicit agreement with the major airlines. But who actually buys stuff in airports? I've never purchased anything other than Rolaids, gum, a shrink-wrapped porno mag, or a newspaper; never a suitcase, briefcase, T-shirt, or bottle of Chanel No. 5 at twice the already inflated prices (though I do take home a duty-free litre of Canadian whiskey whenever traveling back from the Great White North). Of all the shops, restaurants, and services at DFW, I'm willing to bet McDonald's rakes in the most cash, perhaps nearly as much as the hotels in Vegas, spitting out Big Macs that way slots do quarters. Taco Bell runs a close second. I have to admit, in my years of flying out of DFW, the food has improved, though at the expense of some of the best local refried beans I ever tasted.

Call me Whitman of the air terminal. The whole embrace-able world can pass by in a place as big as DFW, just as it can in a city such as Las Vegas. If Vegas is the city of the American dream, then most folks will eventually get there. But first they might consider what to wear. I am reminded of an article I read a number of years ago, where a writer complained about the lack of an airline dress code, how in recent times he noticed a decline in passenger attire. He bemoaned the relaxed dress of yuppies in permanent press, lambasted those in blue jeans and T-shirts, and, God forbid, swore off those in shorts too short or too tight for public display—and I would add to the list those whose bared bellies are best never seen. It seems attire changes with the economy. In a bull market, people take more liberty with fashion; in a bear market, they cover up. Then there are those, like the woman across from me wearing a yellow Easter bonnet, who simply have no concept of style. She's a rotund, middle-aged gal with gold-painted toenails in blue plastic sandals. Such a bonnet will never withstand the strong, dry winds of a Vegas summer, but I'm sure the toenails will be a hit poolside. I feel nonetheless a bond with her, an understanding of why we're all on this evening junket with the cowboy and banker, the attorney and accountant, the wannabe model with long ivory legs (Heartattack!) and our pilot, Malibu Ken. We have a common goal, and if they hit it big before me, I'll be sure to cheer for them.

Malibu Ken in the stars-and-stripes tie is a tall, blond fellow with a muscular build, who looks more fit for Venice Beach than the helm of our airboat to Las Vegas. If we were going to LAX, I'd almost expect a pilot like him, but we're going to Vegas and the crew needs to look more serious than the passengers. His companions, in freshly pressed blue slacks and crisp white shirts, however, look more professional, making me feel the confidence I need when boarding a metal can that flies nearly five miles above ground. Even their epaulets—a word I don't get to use often—are perfectly straight. The stewardesses, or flight attendants now, seem a bit bland in their blue slacks or knee-length blue skirts with white blouses, except for the one wearing the teasing silk neck scarf. I remember a time years ago when sexy stewardess seemed almost a cliché. I could get on a Pan Am flight in frosty Chicago and fall in love before I landed in tropical Miami. Changes in the industry, in the country for that matter, have made sexy almost a crime—what happened to playful slogans spilling over with sexual innuendo, "Coffee, tea, or a flick of my Bic?" Certainly, changes in the language have helped some of us to realize the necessity of developing a social conscience; then again there are also those Puritans at heart, ready to board a plane to paradox.

Just less than 24 hours ago, I signed off on my grade sheet from my summer seminar on "American Literature from Walt Whitman to Raymond Carver." For four steamy weeks, I sat with six young women for two and a half hours a day, reading the hallmarks of our literary tradition. I feigned being the professor they seemed to desire, except for the tweed jacket because of the temperature and humidity in the high nineties. I think of them tonight because, even with their newly acquired knowledge of how to read texts, they were probably not the least wise to my alter ego in our Bible Belt town—Pabst drinker, craps player, vodka swizzler, advocate for legalization, and a guy who once sat front row with his father to watch Suzanne Somers sing in a topless revue. (This last fact I used to brag about in college, though now it seems more typical Vegas camp than anything else.) Tonight, more than any day in class, I feel the spirit of Walt Whitman, the bard who settled in Camden who my New Jersey grandfather called a bit "funny," but not in the humorous sense. I want to reach out to my fellow passengers, even the woman with the gold toenails, and join hands together. We all desire the ching-ching of money in the pan, to carry a plastic bucket heavy with coins in one hand while balancing a watered-down cocktail in the other. We're no different than the Forty-niners who went west before us, only we can arrive faster now than by covered wagon. The dream of seeing the elephant still lives, burning in each of us tonight, as it did for Frank Norris's McTeague in Death Valley. Whitman would have loved Vegas, would have marveled at the lights, the glitz, the sequins, the music of Liberace, the drag revue. He would have wanted to kiss those on skid row, the seamy underside of this city of American lights. In Vegas, there is something for everybody, and for the right price, all desire shall be quenched—I am mad to be in contact with it.

Venus rising from a half-shell, Vegas appears like fortune herself. Going to Vegas is my time to forget the grind of grading hundreds of poorly written papers, the snotty suburban kids with pierced noses and red sneakers who think I'm there to coddle them, those who would rather smoke dope than attend my classes, and young women with tattooed roses on their backsides—where do you position yourself to appreciate such art? Such are the fancies of university life from which I make my yearly summer escape—and I haven't even talked about the faculty! Little do such students know that, even with my eight years of postbaccalaureate education, twice that of your average lawyer, I'm perpetually underpaid and overworked in an overcrowded classroom. Although I open minds (at least I have the fantasy that I do), provide opportunity and the tools to successful life in business and the community, my work goes on silently. For those who say that education costs too much these days, think again; it doesn't cost enough. Salaries are too low, and facilities are deteriorating faster than our crumbling highways. Education is a privilege treated like common admission to the Saturday matinee. Institutions across the country exploit graduate students for their cheap labor, denying them health care and paying them subsistence wages at best—migrant workers employed in my town's slaughterhouse make a better living and have better coverage. I've been on a committee whose members, during a budget crisis, suggested paying graduate teachers even less, perhaps so faculty would have the labor pool necessary not to have to teach those classes themselves. The system is in crisis and further weakening can only result in our nation losing its intellectual and technological edge, though my Marxist colleague would say it's already lost. The gap being created will eventually become a chasm.

In seeking temporary salvation from the rigors of life, I'm not alone. Each year, while Vegas constructs more and more hotel rooms, the prices of those rooms continue to climb. It seems like market economics in reverse. In our capitalist country, something might appear drastically wrong. The answer might be that demand continues to increase, even as casino betting has proliferated across the country. Why Vegas? Why do we keep coming to this city where bellboys used to light my cigarette—when I used to smoke—and hand me a drink when I stepped into the casino? The quality of service has certainly suffered in recent years, the crowds bigger every summer. My love of Vegas I recognize as an ideological contradiction within me—I hate crowds, secondhand smoke, buffet food, and leisure suits, yet I love spectacle, neon, slot machines, prime rib with plenty of horseradish, high heels and fishnet stockings (Heart-attack!). Perhaps Vegas, grown from the criminal dreams and financial forethought of Bugsy Siegel and Meyer Lansky, who opened the Flamingo in 1946, represents my subconscious capitulation to capitalist consumer culture, a once-a-year ben-der, an enema to wash out the Puritan within, something that needs to exist to remind us of why we wouldn't want the rest of the country to be this way, supersized and infantilized into the overstimulated, overweight, and cholesterol-challenged.

I still vividly remember my first trip to Vegas. I was a mea-ger 120-pound eighteen-year-old with a pencil mustache, who looked more fit to star in child porn than pose as a big-time gambler. Back then it seemed they let anyone through the door, the casinos treating me with the adult respect given to every able-bodied gambler, even the underaged. I wasn't alone. Three others traveled with me from Chicago in a Jeep CJ that my buddy won in a lottery. We had already been gone a week, free-wheeling our way across the country with no particular desti-nation. It seemed we stopped in every bar and liquor store west of the Mississippi, not to mention smoked enough dope to ensure the stability of the Mexican economy. In my duffel, I brought along a copy of Hunter S. Thompson's *Fear and Loathing* and another friend was reading Kerouac's *On the Road*. Perhaps we should have brought a Bible.

We had been driving all day from the highs of the Colorado Rockies. I wanted to go find John Denver's home but my bud-dies insisted we drive out to Vegas. Utah that day seemed like it might never end, and there certainly weren't enough liquor stores along the way. Most of the time, we were the only ones on the highway. To a bunch of boys from the flatlands of Illinois, the red rocks and canyon lands were truly unbelievable, as if we were on another planet, which wasn't too much of a stretch in Utah. The more we drove, the more it seemed as if the desert might never end. We followed the setting sun into Arizona toward the Nevada border. I remember the night falling upon us, the way the entire world seemed to darken except for our headlights. I might never have been in a darker place than that desert that night. We continued driving, planning to spend the evening in Vegas and move on to Los Angeles in the morning. We drove and we drove, the miles of that day longer with each passing hour until, out of the middle of nowhere, the desert bloomed with light—yellows, blues, pinks. The closer we came, the brighter these lights grew. From the darkness of the surrounding desert, Vegas appeared to us as a promised land. I'll never forget descending into the valley, then driving down the Strip, which beckoned to us the way ports of call do sailors. Billboards advertised for that $.99 steak and egg breakfast. There were signs for the $4.99 prime rib special, $1.00 Heinekens, all-nude revues. It was everything teenaged boys traveling all day through a desert could ever want. And when the bellhop at the Stardust offered me cigarettes, I knew I had found a place I would be returning to for the rest of my life.

I could go on, tell of the other truly amazing things I discovered in the desert—how I washed my laundry in the tub of the cheap digs of the now-demolished Jamaica Inn; how my pants that day in the hundred-and-fifteen-degree heat took only five minutes to dry after I hung them off the balcony railing; how my buddy found $400 in traveler's checks stashed under his motel mattress, then forged the signatures and lost the cash playing poker with the sharks; how playing only one quarter in the slots I hit the jackpot, but because I didn't play the maximum number of quarters, I didn't receive the $10,000 in cash (Heartattack!); how it happened to me three more times when I was low on quarters and playing the minimum—*heartattack, heartattack, heartattack*—until I lost all the money I brought with me for the trip trying to hit it yet another time; how in the bathroom stall, in one of the lowest moments of my ethical life, I contemplated mugging the Japanese tourist taking a crap next to me, until I remembered the hidden cameras and my dear mother.

Nowadays, it's hard to imagine scientists once performed atomic tests only miles away from the Strip where I lost it all. To view the blasts, casinos offered picnic trips, as they do now to see Hoover Dam. A tourist could even take home bits of rock blown away by the forces of an invisible god. The city continues to offer amazing sights today. In many restrooms of the best hotels, there are still bathroom attendants to offer a towel, shine shoes, or wipe away your drips. It's a dying tradition throughout the rest of the country, a last vestige of an era when service meant something important to hotel guests. It seems today that, with more and more uncouth travelers taking to the road, service is in dire jeopardy. Such tourists don't seem to appreciate having a fellow around to watch you pee. These inexperienced travelers are people who wait for hours to eat at buffets or cook on hotplates in their room, even making grilled cheese with housekeeping's irons—I'm not making this up. These are folks who saw *Titanic* and liked it, then went back five or six times.

While many things are changing in Sin City these days, Vegas still has pretty girls. In the politically correct environment on the campus where I teach, such a statement might be considered harassment by some, but to the discerning traveler in Las Vegas, it's plainly the truth. I'm sure most of these girls come from small towns, places like Independence, Kansas, where almost every teen dreams about the day she gets out. I can picture them at the bus stop, suitcase in hand, a few dollars in their pockets, not knowing which way to the Strip, something out of a William Inge drama. Some with ample bosoms and coordination will find work in one of the rigorous dance shows. Others who can't dance end up a few blocks over at the nudie bars. Those with no talent hustle drinks or take up the oldest of professions. The fresh faces are the ones who haven't been long in town, others have faces so weathered you have to take it on faith they once were lovely. For lack of a more fitting term, such hags with gravelly, whiskey-pickled voices and a smoker's hack are wise old birds. They work as buffet hostesses or make change. Some have even made their way into positions of power, coordinating the fresh faces, making sure they fill an entire tray with drinks before returning to the craps table.

I have no doubt these women, young and old, stay with their jobs because the tips are good, especially at tables kissed by luck. These flowers of the desert night become tip junkies, going home at the end of their shifts with wads of cash and dreams of the next day's fistful of dollars. Making money hustling vodka tonics to the rude and crude, to ass-ogling corporate execs on the lam, becomes an addiction, a cycle too difficult to break when the next best job is selling tacos or burgers at minimum wage. The math is simple, if not enslaving. Those gals who rise above the slosh, waggling their way night after night from table to table, are the truly gifted. I want to embrace these remarkable women, broads in stiletto heels, girls with more smile than a toothpaste model, women with gifted anatomy of inspiring proportions, the envy of starving teenagers across America. They are as much a part of the dream and fantasy of Vegas as Snow White and Cinderella are to Disneyland—and better tipped. I wish to thank them collectively for the satisfying sneak peaks, for their countless hours spent at indoor health clubs on ass-trimming treadmills. For what these women go through—pinches from dirty old men, cosmetics bills as costly as my monthly groceries, the pain of plastic surgery, aching tits from tight bras, feet sore from hours of moving among the slot zombies—they deserve every last cent of their hard-earned nightly cash.

I have been to Sin City so often over the years I've lost count. I've forgotten how much I've lost but remember the way dice fly out of the hand, the tableside taste of vodka with a lemon twist, every heart attack. Throughout my college years at the University of California in San Diego, Vegas made for a cheap and convenient getaway. I would even go on occasion to spend time with one or both of my parents, a tradition I occasionally continue on my yearly pilgrimages, always bringing along my bingo dauber for those slow daytime hours with Mom. I like to stay at hotels like Bally's or MGM, quality rooms at slightly inflated prices. I was once tempted by a cheap room offer and burned, my wife and I given a basement room with soiled red shag at the old Aladdin's, where just down the hall a room of chain-smoking Vietnamese men stayed up all night playing poker. On a bed with a padded and dented headboard, we slept that night fully clothed with our shoes on and didn't bother to stay for the buffet in the morning. When ensconced at a quality hotel, I tend to have some of my best sleep high above the lights and groan of continuous traffic.

Symbol of my own inner contradictions, as much as I love the town, I don't think that I could ever live there. I feel the same way after spending a week driving about L.A. The hyperactivity boils my nerves, the sun bakes my brain. Just when I think I understand the chemistry of Vegas, it throws me for a loop, as with the demolition of the Sands Hotel. I thought for sure it would be preserved as a legacy to the past, but the past is not a priority in Vegas. It's a city that looks toward the future with a sense of manifest destiny. There are always new plans to build or renovate, plans to expand even when the Strip looks like it can't grow a mile longer and the surrounding mountains seem lost in a blanket of smog. As long as our nation endures, so will its crown jewel of consumer culture, the encapsulation of America's many paradoxes where a Puritan can look the other direction when closing another construction deal.

Tonight, even though the plane is late again at DFW, even though Malibu Ken, our pilot, has a stars-and-stripes tie and a woman with gold toenails sits nearby, I want to join hands for a

Vegas vigil. Together we await the magic with relaxed patience. We know that no matter when we arrive, the city will still be up. There will be steak and eggs at any hour. The cowboy with the black Stetson gives me a friendly nod—"Heartattack, heartattack!" I remind him. Some passengers are already imbibing, others like me reserving our energy for the real festivities. Instead of a ferry crossing a bay, we'll be flying over the U.S. in a Super 80. The Gold Rush never ended in America, nor has the need, instilled in us all from our infancy, to satiate ourselves on a grand scale as only steak-eating Americans like us can. Vegas is our city on the hill, a proving ground in the desert to measure our fate and faith. Even corporate America has become involved, taking over hotels and creating spectacle in a way that seems truly Disneyesque. Boarding the plane, I salute my pilot's tie. He wishes me well. As the bird takes off into the darkness, I wait for the magnificence of those beckoning desert lights, as if somehow it's that very first time again.

THE GREEN BURRITO

I praise the tortilla because I know they
fly into our hands like eager flesh of the one we love,
soft yearnings we delight in biting as we tear
the tortilla and wipe the plate clean.

—Ray Gonzalez, "Praise the Tortilla,
Praise Menudo, Praise Chorizo"

When food and Southern California couple like Gidget and
Moondoggie, what comes about most often are light, fruity dish-
es prepared by fruity chefs—grilled mahi-mahi with an avocado
vinaigrette, pizza topped with a BGH-free organic mozzarella, the
alchemy of Wolfgang Puck. Perhaps the creators of such nou-
velle cuisine even had a hand in the invention of the bikini, a
light, fruity dressing for the body-conscious, SoCal beach girl,
tanned year round the color of a well-roasted Cornish hen. I
lived in Southern California throughout the later half of the
1980s when California cuisine, as it came to be called in finer
establishments I rarely frequented, became as popular as the Jane
Fonda workout. I refer to this period of my life, when I was
young, beautiful, had muscles, lived one block from north San
Diego County's Del Mar beach, and owned a surfboard, as my
brief sojourn in a lost paradise. If a smell can create the
strongest, most powerful and immediate link to memory of any

of our senses, perhaps then the food of Southern California can reconnect me to my glorified past, maybe even to a time before time in the Mesoamerican highlands. During a period before San Diego County's population skyrocketed, before gridlock and smog warnings, before long lines and beach closings due to toxic water, before condos and townhomes sprouted like weeds across the unspoiled coastal hills, I grew fond of black beans with a mango salsa, sushi with inside-out California rolls, alfalfa sprout sandwiches with grape tomatoes on whole wheat bread cooked in a brick oven. However, even as these diets kept up my regularity, I longed for industrial foods found in nuts-and-bolts cities like Chicago, Milwaukee, St. Louis, and Kansas City; I craved meat-heavy, fat-filled, pork-stuffed fare like deep-dish pizza, barbecued ribs, coleslaw, and kosher hot dogs topped with a highly salty condiment such as sauerkraut, pepperoncinis, or pickle relish (preferably the fluorescent green kind).

While in my day, SoCal had its appeal to a youthful, lusty, party-seeking college student like myself, California cuisine was well beyond my meager means. House painting and watering rich folks' indoor plants, two of my more regular types of employment throughout and after my long-awaited graduation, didn't leave much money for dining, especially after that must-purchase case of Schaefer beer. To eat well and often, when my roommates and I weren't scarfing Ramen noodles or mac-n-cheese, we sought out happy-hour buffets and California cuisine of a different sort, a wide-ranging menu of cheap Mexican with SoCal soul I fondly came to call, during a semester of reading Marx and Engels, "the People's Food." It didn't take long before I ate tacos, burritos, and quesadillas as regularly as Pancho Villa or my native SoCal, beach-tanned then-wife-to-be, who grew up with friends of Mexican heritage. In fact, she had eaten such food so often, she even knew what went into a bowl of Sunday menudo.

It was not until I moved back to the Midwest to take up residence in the Little Apple of Manhattan, Kansas, where my auto insurance no longer cost as much as the mortgage on my parents' first home, that I began to long for good Mexican. I craved tacos and burritos served by teenage gals with big dark eyes and rich earthy skin who ran the cash registers and spoke the kitchen's only English—"O for a beaker full of the warm South!" Keats might have lamented. In Manhattan, the only quasi-Mexican food came from two or three sit-down restaurants; one, Carlos O'Kelly's, I remember because it seemed to be named after a leprechaun's illegitimate offspring.

If it weren't for my L.A.-raised, mall-savvy girlfriend (the future wife), whom I convinced about the better life in Kansas the way Pa did Ma in *Little House on the Prairie*, I might never have made it back to SoCal with any frequency to eat and reconnect with my past at some of my favorite Mexican digs. With her family in L.A. and Orange County, I have been assured at least a one-week Mexican eating binge per year, which is probably all a body like mine can take without proper acclimation by regular exposure to food so rich in lard, spice, and spirit. I am on such a binge now.

2 a.m. Kansas time, I'm in L.A., five hours later than expected, about to eat my first Mexican of the day, a bean burrito from my mother-in-law's freezer, which may have been there since my last visit. It's akin to a burrito that can be bought at 7-Elevens across the country twenty-four hours a day. Two microwave minutes later and a healthy dose of Tapatillo hot sauce, its rubbery texture almost tastes good. I eat now only for sustenance, savoring and anticipating the following day when I will begin my burrito-eating tour. Such an eating spree will confirm what I've come to know over the years about the relationship between food and culture in Southern California, perhaps even something about food's ambrosial magic.

To prepare for the heart-clogging, cholesterol-filled bonanza, I have been working out for weeks, eating tofu and keeping away from Kansas beef. I should point out there is heavy pressure in my Kansas town to eat beef as regularly as corn flakes, especially with an IBP slaughterhouse nearby and local ranch hands who drive about with "Eat Beef" license plates affixed to the large front bumpers of their beastly American pickups. While exercising is hard work and foreign to many Kansans, I will, however, go to almost any length to prepare for eating good Mexican without a guilty conscience.

The taco joints of SoCal, as they are regularly called by the locals, come in all shapes and sizes, from a dated strip mall storefront in Orange County to a cinder block shack in San Diego's Del Mar, where it's possible to witness the ongoing battle between land exploitation and conservation all in the same sweeping ocean view. I have been repeatedly coming to some of these joints long enough that trips back to SoCal reflect not only my love of Mexican food but my robust marriage and acceptance into my in-laws' family. In all honesty, lunches and dinners where we hunch together around laminate-topped tables piled high with paper napkins have created a bond between us as with few extended families I know. Such group eating is not, however, entirely foreign to my cultural upbringing. By birth I'm half Italian, the good half I was told, mothered by a full-blood with tomato sauce running through her arteries. I know all about the importance of eating and arguing at family dinner, the prestige of the Old Italian School from which my grandmother graduated, and her regrets for us grandchildren who lacked such a proper education. In Kansas, where my wife, child, and I live alone like pioneers without nearby family, we've grown to miss those dinner gatherings, which in SoCal have been moved from the home to the local taco joint.

In greater Los Angeles, where the phone book lists more Mexican restaurants than my Kansas town has residents, eating out appears to be a religion. In fact, a closer comparison of the yellow pages yields an eerie correspondence between the number of pages of churches in my Kansas town, about three (surely a number of biblical significance), and the number of Mexican restaurants I estimate in L.A., about three thousand (something apocalyptic). In a region of countless intersections, in a state where the highway is art, there can be found near almost every major intersection in greater metropolitan Los Angeles (I conflate here Orange and L.A. counties into one megasprawl) at least one taco joint, and it's likely there are at least two more close by—it's a natural law of the L.A. universe.

The ubiquity of taco joints throughout SoCal reminds me of the once-prevalent pizza and hot dog joints in the Chicago area. While hot dog places have remained numerous, pizza ovens once operated by Italian Americans not long immigrated and naturalized have diminished at an exponential rate. With such a drastically decreasing number of these pizza places, each with its own authentic sauces and pies, the Chicago pizza joint could be put on the endangered restaurants list. Already a large number of these places near my hometown of Northbrook, Illinois, in suburban Chicago have fallen like dominoes (no pun intended). Where once there were deep-dish pies from hot ovens, there are now pizza simulacra from Huts, Godfathers, and Little Caesars wielding imperial dominance. Not even the Mafia can turn this situation around.

While what I have to say is about the burrito, what happened to the pizza is important to consider. Perhaps the disappearance of authentic Chicago pizza in a city that made the pie famous is due more to social causes than hostile corporate takeovers. The first thing to consider is that making pizza, like making good Mexican food, is hard work. It takes countless hours to prepare quality sauces and dough (half Italian, I have firsthand knowledge here), just as it takes a good marinade and plenty of simmer time for the best refried beans, machaca, and carne asada. While a pizza joint may send first- or second-generation Italian Americans to college, few might be willing to return to those long nights in front of a hot oven.

Then there is the dying grandmother syndrome. Without an Italian grandmother's secret recipe or her eight-days-a-week labor in cooking sauces and pinching ravioli, there can be no truly authentic Italian food. Therefore, the theorem that should win me a Nobel prize in food criticism: *the rate of assimilation of Italian Americans into the mainstream is directly proportional to the rate of disappearance of neighborhood pizza joints; similarly, the rate of immigration of Mexican people to Southern California is directly proportional to the rise in taco joints.* A cultural and culinary revolution is born.

The people who own a pizza joint or a taco shack have much in common besides extended families, a love of garlic, hirsute relatives, dashboard statuettes of patron saints, a fondness for votive candles, mustachioed aunts, and firsthand knowledge of a language other than English. While the number of Italian immigrants has steadily declined throughout the twentieth century, the number of Mexican immigrants has steadily increased. Although many throughout the SoCal region worked hard to stem both legal and illegal immigration (even as they continued to drink California wines pressed from grapes gathered by Mexican laborers, dine in restaurants with a Mexican workforce, and consume Central Valley produce picked by migrant workers), a boom in taco joints was taking place around them. While la Migra (the U.S. Border Patrol) stepped up its policing of the border, searching public buses and creating traffic jams at the San Onofre Immigration Checkpoint on the I-5 highway corridor to L.A., the taco revolution silently continued. Little by little, in the same way that pizza crept into suburban TV rooms following World War Two, folks like me found themselves slowly becoming addicted to Mexican food (and frozen burritos in times of need). It remains to be seen if the taco shack will go the way of the authentic pizza joint; however, as more people adopt the taco-eating lifestyle and pledge their allegiance to the burrito, it seems the taco joint might escape danger.

Already ketchup has come to play second fiddle to the delicious combination of hot peppers and tomatoes more commonly known as salsa. Salsa itself might even be the most truly indigenous American food. According to food historian Jean Andrews, for the fascinating *Cambridge World History of Food*, the chili pepper of the genus *Capsicum* was unknown to Europe and Asia until Columbus's 1492 voyage—no Hungarian goulash, no Madras curries, no kung pao chicken, no spicy Thai, no Malaysian biryani existed before Columbus, except in their blander forms. The tomato, too, hails from the Americas. A variety of the wild tomato similar to the stringy and often intractable cherry tomato most likely originated somewhere near Peru. *Cambridge's* Janet Long notes how tomato seeds disseminated on strong winds or with the help of birds. Eventually the fruit became domesticated in the Puebla–Veracruz area of Mexico a few thousand years ago. The word "tomato" itself, a Spanish variation, comes from the Nahuatl *tomatl*, and tomatoes were readily available in various strains in the Tlatelolco market in Tenochtitlán in 1519. The Aztecs, as conquistador Bernal Díaz del Castillo reported in his *Historia Verdadera de la Conquista de la Nueva España*, often spiced their human sacrifices with a salsa of chili peppers, tomatoes, and salt. I might add that it's perhaps an ironic coincidence that, according to L. Patrick Coyle's *World Encyclopedia of Food*, Northern Europeans, including those in the British Isles, avoided tomatoes, believing them to be poisonous, as the tomato is a relative of the belladonna, or deadly nightshade. As Coyle warns, it's imperative to eat only the fruit, avoiding tomato leaves for their toxicity.

Without a doubt, Mexican food has changed American culture in the same way pizza, the hamburger, and the hot dog did for earlier generations. If my own icebox back home is any example, the revolution has now made its way to Kansas. Hot sauces in my refrigerator: La Victoria Salsa Brava Hot, La Victoria Green Taco Sauce Mild, Tamazula Salsa Picante ("Mexican Hot Sauce" says the label), Herdez Salsa Casera (México's Favorite! House Salsa), Pace Picante Hot, Trappey's Red Devil Cayenne Pepper Sauce, Louisiana's Pure Crystal Hot

Sauce, Chi-Chi's Restaurante Fiesta Salsa Medium, Tabasco Brand Pepper Sauce, as well as two onions, three jalepeños, two packs of Mission Flour Tortillas, and a stack of Mission Corn Tortillas, 24 count.

Throughout my first day at my SoCal in-laws', I've thought about little but our evening trip to Rubi's Frosty Freeze in Whittier, a town home to the green burrito of all green burritos and former President Richard Nixon. We leave the house about the same time the sun begins to cast a warm pink glow over the San Gabriel Mountains to the east (hills to locals not from Kansas). We're a big crew, so we drive up in two cars to the corner of Whittier's Broadway and Washington. This mixed neighborhood, where Spanish is spoken as frequently as English, is typical taco territory, part residential, part industrial, mostly SoCal concrete. Just up the road is a Pep Boys auto shop and across the street on Broadway, an abandoned bowling alley being demolished to build a strip mall. On the corner is a liquor store and currency exchange, also slated for demolition. Kitty-corner is Chris'-n-Pitt's barbecue with a parking lot full of cars (my mother-in-law claims the food was good fifteen years ago when she last ate there). Next to the BBQ joint is a place calling itself "The Embers," a dimly lit lounge that sports few customers taking advantage of its many parking spaces; it's the kind of dive that without my family with me I might venture into just to say I've been there. Across on Washington, people fill their SUVs at a Shell station, and, right behind Rubi's, there is a small beauty salon calling itself simply "Hair & Nail Design" (and something just beneath in Korean I can't make out, perhaps a catchier name). On this corner, the American Dream makes its last stand. It's still possible here to buy any of three newspapers for a mere quarter before hopping the #270 Metro Bus to Monrovia via El Monte Station. Even Superman can change in a flash using what must be one of the last remaining glass phone booths in the United States just outside Rubi's front doors.

Upon entering, it's possible to feel from the dated decor that you're going back in time while moving forward with the taco revolution. Inside the Grade B–inspected kitchen, grandmothers in hairnets prepare the food from time-tested recipes; Rubi's itself boasts being "family owned and operated since 1969." Working the counter are the requisite teen beauties, who take orders and fill dreams with eyes of polished agate and bodies supple as young palms. The menu is fueled with heartbusting goodness: tacos, burritos, and quesadillas, as well as hamburgers, hot dogs, sandwiches, and fries. It's an integrated menu, much like the neighborhood itself. The food at most taco joints is just this basic, with the variety and uniqueness of taste found in the differing recipes. I compare the difference to the way my mother's and grandmother's Abruzzi spaghetti little resembles a woman's from Naples. A few days later, when I eat at the ocean-view Roberto's in Del Mar some one hundred highway miles south, there will be few changes to the basic menu but the tastes will be as different as competing brands of hot sauce.

A taco joint is not only food. Most neighborhood eateries can boast at least one video machine. Rubi's has ten such machines, including the popular Mortal Combat, Spy Hunter, and NBA Jam. At Rubi's, even the most anachronistic of us can feel comforted by the aged wall paneling, dusty plastic plants, wall-mounted TV, and vinyl-covered booths with laminate-topped tables. If you were from Mexico, you'd feel at home with advertising for Olé, "Mexico's favorite drink," made from rice and milk. And although the kitchen only received a B rating, all customers could feel secure in knowing that the owner received an "American Food Safety Institute Certificate of Completion" that is "certified by Anthony W. Mitchell, Ph.D."

If that's not enough to whet the appetite, the hot sauce will. With its selections of mild, medium, and hot, as well as salsa fresca and green salsa, there is a regard for hot sauces at Rubi's only true lovers of Mexican can appreciate. It's a celebration of piquant condiments and the culture of food I've encountered only a few times, in places such as Albuquerque, New Orleans, and Baton Rouge, where the LSU cafeteria served students gumbo, fried catfish, hush puppies, and étouffée, not to mention gave them a choice of two types of coffee, regular and chicory, and two hot sauces on every cafeteria table. Surely, the hallmark of a great culture is its culinary products.

Looking over the menu, I make an easy decision and order the green burrito, an extraordinary combination of creamy refried beans cooked in lard then mixed with green chilies before being wrapped like a baby in a warm flour tortilla. A future Miss Whittier with obsidian hair takes my order, then, along with a slew of hungry locals leaning against the long front window, I wait for my number to be called. Unlike fast-food places that can stuff a sack full of hamburgers in less than a minute, good Mexican takes time to prepare. I watch las abuelas in the kitchen prepare our orders, steam rising from the grill into their wrinkled faces. In the air is the scent of frying potatoes and stewing chilies. Miss Whittier—who probably has no idea who Richard Nixon was and who never has, unlike me, visited the Nixon library, where myth trumps history—smiles at every customer. When she finally calls my number, I thank her for my burrito rolled tightly in white paper, then quickly join my in-laws at our usual corner table, some already eating while the food is still warm. With a dip of my burrito in a pool of red hot sauce, the hottest of the many sauces, I can only hope the food of angels is the Rubi's green burrito—*How blessed I am.*

If Rubi's is the measure of all taco joints, a community center and cultural legacy, then other taco joints might be measured by their deviation from its norm. I can't help but indulge myself further here, as I feel I have become much more than a mere observer of taco culture and a critic of the burrito. Before continuing, I should digress only momentarily to point out how, just across the border, the cuisine and presentation vary widely. On Tijuana's Avenida Revolución street, vendors sell tacos from pushcarts. A longstanding rumor or American cultural prejudice has suggested their use of dog or horse meat as filler. Nonetheless, due to loose hygienic standards, eating from a Tijuana street vendor isn't something I advocate because of the potential for serious health risks; a Del Mar neighbor of mine once claimed he caught hepatitis from such tacos. In more formal restaurants across the border and down the Baja coast, the lobster taco is common. I can further boast about some of the best enchiladas of my life in Cuernavaca, an extraordinary quesadilla in Cancún, and some bitter Dramamine after a bus trip up the mountains outside Mexico City to the silver-mining town of Taxco.

When I lived near the border, I had numerous opportunities to observe the importance of the tortilla in Mexican daily life, especially on my many trips to Mexico either for humanitarian purposes or to indulge in excessive drink like an ugly American or common seaman on leave. I once volunteered to help build latrines in the ghettos known as Tijuana's Colonias, and on such trips often visited the local tortilléria to purchase a stack of unrivaled, fresh corn tortillas for the equivalent of a dime back in the States but a day's wage in Tijuana. Whenever I bite into a tortilla, I can't help but think I'm connecting with the age of the great Maya and Aztec cultures before the continuing Conquest, when maize, squash, beans, tomatoes, and chilies made up a large portion of the Mesoamerican diet. As Ellen Messer describes, some of the first traces of cultivated maize, 7,000 to 10,000 years ago, have come from a cave near Tehuacán Puebla in central Mexico. She estimates that maize cultivation reached North America between 600 and 11,000 A.D. Interestingly, John C. Super and Louis Alberto Vargas note, in their overview, "The History and Culture of Food and

Drink in the Americas," that in the Guatemalan highlands, the Quiché Maya word for maize is *kana*, which can be translated as "our mother." With maize came the tortilla, often eaten with beans, which together provided a mix of proteins similar to animal sources.

Maize becomes a tortilla through a series of steps that begins with soaking the corn kernels in lime until the skin comes off. After grinding and the addition of water, the mixture known as mixtamal can be rolled into balls that are typically pressed flat in a hot pan or with a tortilla iron. Not until the Spanish introduced wheat, or harina, into the New World was the flour tortilla born. As wheat cultivation itself flourished in North America, such tortillas became known as tortillas de harina del norte (tortillas of wheat from the north) or tortillas de harina fronterizas (frontier-style tortillas of wheat). The collision of cultures in Mexico created what we know today as Mexican food. Local cultures contributed the beans and salsa (tomatoes and chilies), and the Spanish added not only wheat, but pigs, sheep, and cattle from which cheese, butter, and lard could be produced. The Spaniards also brought the onions, garlic, and rice that would become staples of many Mexican meals, and they introduced frying, typically in lard but sometimes in olive oil, that made possible frijoles refritos, or refried beans.

After building outhouses under a hot Mexican sun, I was regularly invited to dine with the families I had helped, a home cooking second only to my mother's spaghetti, a reward more than ample for my time. In Mexico, I discovered the family meal was still the most important moment of the day, a moment to pocket everyone's ideologies and cultural misunderstandings, to celebrate the blessing of food itself. Even when pesos are scarce, eating well means something elemental—"Pay the butcher, not the doctor," my Italian-speaking nana always said. I can only lament that, for many American families who rush to and from work, dance lessons, tap, piano, football, baseball, soccer, basketball, karate, swimming, tennis, volleyball, track,

PTO, Boy Scouts, Girl Scouts, 4-H, the orthodontist, or the mall (I know I left something out), family dinner has grown less important. However, in Mexico, as in Italy, eating together and well remains sacrosanct. Just the memory of sharing creamy refried beans and tortillas heated over an open flame from a worn-out propane burner in a squatter's shack with no electricity, cardboard walls, and a roof of discarded metal sheeting, makes me understand that, yes, I have at times lived deliberately—*How blessed I am.*

After Rubi's, I find myself the next night indulging on Mexican again at Baja Fresh in Brea. Baja Fresh, like the recently gentrified Brea, is an upscale taco joint. At Baja Fresh, now a burgeoning franchise across America, there are bright lights, new tables, and a menu that boasts black beans. In surveying the offerings, I find the standard fare described using a California-cuisine vocabulary—grilled, steamed, sautéed—which is unusual for the typically lard-heavy, fried food of most taco joints, though the descriptions do have a mouthwatering effect. Unlike the more urban clientele at Rubi's, where Bus #270 passes regularly, the people at Baja Fresh, in shorts, sandals, and Hawaiian shirts, who burp their car alarms before entering, seem to have just come from the backyard pool (and they probably did).

After a long period of indecision, when I can feel the tension mounting in the growing line behind me, I finally order a grilled chicken burrito stuffed with beans and rice topped with avocado and a cilantro-heavy salsa. My only trouble is deciding what type of hot sauce to choose from the hot sauce buffet; I settle, again, for the hottest sauce, which will make my nose run (a good test for measuring hot sauce heat). The chicken has a nice grilled flavor and the tortilla is fresh. The pinto beans are, unexpectedly, not refried but whole and lack some flavor. The sauce, while hot, could have a fuller flavor, too, but altogether the burrito is as good as a franchise burrito can be, making Taco Bell seem like taco hell. When I'm finished stuffing myself, I feel like asking the tan, good-looking young couple next to us if they wouldn't mind if I went back to their pool for a dip. Then again, I'm so full I'd probably sink.

There is no room to describe in detail every place I've eaten Mexican on this trip, but I should say that on day three I went to Garduno's Dos Amigo in La Mirada, notable for its adjacent carnicería, or meat market—*How blessed I am*—and on day four, I found myself at Rubio's Baja Grill—*How blessed I am*— not to be confused with Rubi's Tasty Freeze in Whittier. Rubio's Baja Grill boasts of being "Home of the Fish Taco." Rubio's has seventy-three SoCal locations, a number that might sound astronomical in Kansas but, if you know about SoCal's exponential growth, is not that surprising.

Today, my fifth, I'm back in Whittier again, this time at A Taste of Mexico, a unique joint serving a different kind of community than most. A Taste of Mexico is just up the road from my in-laws', off La Mirada Boulevard. It's July and the city of La Mirada has up its streetlamp banners with presidential portraits. Even Bill Clinton and Richard Nixon get a lamp, their banners showing no signs of tampering. Along this road of presidential smiles, American assimilation has been redefined. A billboard for Coors Light advertises, *Refresca tu sed de fútbol* (Refresh your thirst from soccer), and another for Kern's juice, *Ahora con calcio* (Now with calcium). The placards make me want to call up my high-school Spanish teachers, Señor Austin and Señora Guerrero, to thank them for giving me an exceptional education in the Spanish language. Years ago, when I dreamed more of undoing bras than success in Spanish class, I never predicted how useful a second language could be in America, especially as my lust for burritos substitutes for lustfulness itself at this point in my life.

To add to the excitement and my patriotic sentiment stirred by the two Roosevelt banners and JFK's courageous presidential profile, it's my first visit to A Taste of Mexico. First visits to new taco joints can be exciting but also gastronomically risky. However, the search for new and better tacos overrides my fear of indigestion and diarrhea. A Taste of Mexico is in an aged strip mall. The storefronts seem old and weathered by California standards, where new buildings and shopping centers multiply like automobiles on the L.A. freeway. Just next door is a "Coin-Op" laundry, "Free Dry with Wash," making me lament I did not bring a sack of dirty clothes.

Before I even walk into A Taste of Mexico, I'm already not impressed with its name. The best taco joints are named after people, perhaps their owners or family members. I've already been to Rubi's, Gardunos, and Rubio's, and I can still try, within a few blocks, Arturo's Puffy Taco, Casa Cisneros, Casa Gamino, Casa Martinez, La Casa Garcia, Los Sanchez, Joaquin's, and Villa Hernandez. I've come to A Taste of Mexico with my brother-in-law, Tommy, who swears that not only is the food good but the portions large, which is enough of a recommendation for me to overcome my prejudice toward the lousy name. It's just such word of mouth that builds taco-joint reputations, especially in strip malls where an Abe's Automotive Repair implicitly promises an honest mechanic.

Compared to the capaciousness of Rubi's, with its room for ten video machines, A Taste of Mexico has only two such games: Galaga and Street Fighter. The place seems oddly shaped, with more depth than width. Booths along the wall are fronted with arches painted with vines that seem stolen from the set of a bad Italian opera (perhaps this used to be a pizza joint); the wooden latticework in the front window begs me to wonder about the intentions of the interior designer. The unusual decor, a phrase that seems redundant in describing taco joints, is topped only by the counter's display of lollipops, Lemonheads, Acirrico Chili Powder, Lucas Limon Powdered Salt, and phone cards. *Phone cards?*

It's the cards more than the chili powder and lemon salt that lead me to realize that A Taste of Mexico serves a much different clientele than the suburbanites who frequent Baja Fresh or Rubi's assimilated, urban patrons. I know about these phone cards because, back in Kansas, our immigrant slaughter-house laborers (nonunion) use them to call family in Mexico. I imagine it's no different at A Taste of Mexico, whose name tries too hard to interest gringos.

The menu at A Taste of Mexico also reflects its immigrant tastes. Besides the standard taco-joint fare, A Taste of Mexico serves such taco-joint oddities as shrimp bread, shrimp devil (an inviting combo of shrimp with tomato, onion, and cilantro), chile verde (pork and green chili), lengua tacos (beef tongue), menudo (tripe soup), posole (pork and corn soup), and albondigas (meatballs). All of this can be washed down with Jarritos, Orchata, Jamaica, or Tamarindo, favorite Mexican soft drinks. Such fare might send the average white dude running for his Tagamet. Even though I will be traveling in the morning, I risk possible intestinal complications and order the chile verde, a favorite dish of mine I usually eat only in New Mexico. Behind the counter, the dreamboat with big brown eyes takes my order, which will be prepared by the old ladies in the kitchen under the direction, as the sign indicates, of "Chef Fidel Renteria." Before I have time to watch the neighborhood kids finish an innocent game of Street Fighter, my food is ready to go in large Styrofoam containers with "Have a Nice Day" embossed on the lid.

For a mere $4.95, I receive a large portion of chile verde, a stack of warm corn tortillas, a hefty bowl of menudo (which I will try for my first time), and rice and beans. On my way out the door, carrying large plastic sacks heavy with food destined for my hungry in-laws, I'm almost tempted to buy a phone card or a shaker of lemon salt to take back to Kansas.

At the in-laws', I applaud Tommy for his recommendation. A tall, husky blond who could do Hungry Jack commercials, he's an expert on many things Southern Californian, from

Disneyland to freeway traffic patterns, and he knows his Mexican. The chile verde is delicious, the best I've had outside New Mexico—*How blessed I am.* Tommy insists I try the menudo, too, though he does so with chagrin. My in-laws all curiously watch me taste menudo for my first time; though the tripe is a bit on the slimy side, the soup has a peppery and slightly salty flavor ... not bad! My mother-in-law says menudo is a good cure for hangovers, a fact I vow to remember, tequila being one of my favorite drinks. My wife admits she hasn't eaten menudo since childhood at the dinner tables of her Mexican friends; back then she secretly spit the guts into her napkin, then covertly stuffed it all into her pocket. Such are the sacrifices of a gringo in paradise.

It might seem almost impossible to top my last few days of Mexican indulgence were it not for a short trip down the coast to the Roberto's on Del Mar's Carmel Valley Road across the lagoon from the Torrey Pines State Beach just north of San Diego. Roberto's is a taco shack sans pareil, if I may borrow from the French. Twenty people back in the lunch line, I wait to order for my wife, child, and mother-in-law. Maybe it's the salt air and the smell of grilling asada beef that causes me to flash back fifteen years to my youthful college days in this sleepy seaside town made famous by Jimmy Durante and his horse racing pals. Roberto's, unlike me, has changed little in twenty years, so little I begin to think that I can take my sack of burritos back to my old beach house, then surf away the afternoon in the warm sunshine: same orange, sun-faded tabletops, same small patio overlooking the state beach and coastal lagoon, same million-dollar homes just up the street, same yuppies with fashionable sunglasses and leased sports cars, same superficial blondes with enhanced breasts in see-through beach wraps. Without a doubt, Roberto's is taco paradise, "Where the Surf Meets the Turf," as they say about the Del Mar horse track.

Unlike A Taste of Mexico, the menu at Roberto's is simple: burritos, tacos, enchiladas, quesadillas. When I come to Roberto's, I always, always, have a carne asada, and sometimes a quesadilla stuffed with, by request, Spanish rice, a serendipitous combination I discovered one afternoon in college when I had the munchies. Until I finally get to place our orders, I pass the time reminiscing about the good old days living in a town with incomparable Mexican, before marriage, a child, debt, and a move to Kansas that still surprises my old friends. I watch the enhanced blondes in front of me jiggle their way to the front of the line, and some fifteen minutes later, I pick up my white sack of food (still the same) and grab eight small plastic containers of hot sauce (still the same).

How blessed I am, I think, as I sit down with my family at a familiar orange table with an ocean view. We are surrounded by pigeons raised on Roberto's waiting for a generous crumb; gulls squawk at us in their passing. I stare out at the sea shimmering a beckoning blue in the distance. For a moment, the briefest of moments, I actually feel like I'm in college again—nineteen and tan, fit and lusty. A nice ocean breeze blows off the breaking surf—*How blessed I am*. It's surely the smell of warm tortillas and grilled asada beef that triggers these memories, the way the right combination of Italian spices brings to me the voice of my grandmother. Food is something magical, something powerful. Food, I become certain, can liberate, its smell the strongest link to our pasts. For another brief moment, I forget I exist in any dimension other than the now, this moment of moments, here at my favorite taco joint in the entire world. With a wave of my napkin, I whisk away the crumbs of a previous indulgence. I unwrap my burrito, dip it in hot sauce, then take that first incredible bite—O, O, O! *How blessed I am!* Just as I remembered—the entire world still in its proper place, at least for today.

Perhaps on this corner, there's a special alignment of sun and moon, call it taco-shack feng shui. In the distance, waves break along the shore as they have for uninterrupted eons—

How blessed I am. The enhanced blondes, now seated at the table beside me, seem to smile my way and I smile back—*How blessed I am.* The next day, like Dorothy, I'll find myself back in Kansas, wondering who controls the magic, waiting for the taco revolution to continue spreading east like the wind. I might not make it back to Roberto's for a year or more—god forbid, maybe never again. Roberto's might not even be here the next time I come, another victim of continuing California sprawl. I don't want to get up and try not to think about that fateful day when my glorified past will become a condo development, when Mexican goes the way of the endangered authentic deep-dish pizza. We'll share a divine hour at our orange table that will last long after the trip ends, when the echo of the surf turns to a lonely wind on an empty prairie. I take another bite of my burrito—*blessed, blessed, blessed.* Before I click my heels three times, I try to make this loveliest of moments last, take it all in … everything … as far as I can go.

The Green Burrito
(my own recipe and rival to the Rubi's original)

Ingredients
1 1/2 cups uncooked pinto beans
2–3 quarts water
3 cloves garlic
1/2 teaspoon salt, divided
6 tablespoons lard, bacon grease, or olive oil. Increase if desired.
8–10 ounces fire-roasted New Mexico or Anaheim chilies, peeled and seeded
4 large flour tortillas
Sour cream, cheddar or jack cheese, and salsa (for toppings)
Hot sauce

Wash beans and soak overnight. Drain.

Put beans, 2–3 quarts water, 1 smashed garlic clove, and 1/4 teaspoon of salt into a heavy pot. Bring to boil and simmer 1 1/2 to 2 hours, or until beans soften. (If you forget to soak your beans overnight or wish to cook them while doing other chores, you can place beans in a Crock-Pot with the water, garlic and salt, then simmer on high for 4 to 5 hours.)

Drain and set aside about 3 cups of cooked beans.

In a cast-iron pan, melt lard or heat olive oil (lard or bacon grease will provide more flavor). Add chilies and remaining 2 cloves of pressed garlic. Sauté for 3–5 minutes over low flame. Add more lard or oil, if necessary.

Add the 3 cups of cooked beans, then mash. Fry mashed beans with chilies in oil over low heat 1–3 minutes, then slowly add a few teaspoons of water until the mashed beans take on a creamy texture. Cook to desired consistency. Salt to taste with remaining 1/4 teaspoon of salt. Simmer 3 to 5 minutes, or keep warm until ready to serve.

Warm tortillas in another pan, or in microwave, then fill tortillas with green chili and refried bean mixture. Top, if desired, with sour cream, jack or cheddar cheese, and/or your favorite salsa.

Roll each tortilla into a burrito, then serve with plenty of hot sauce.

Serves four.

O PARADISE!
A Pastoral

I.

vola con li occhi per questo giardino;
ché veder lui t'acconcerà lo sguardo
più al montar per lo raggio divino.

Fly with thine eyes all round about this garden;
For seeing it will discipline thy sight
Farther to mount along the ray divine.

—Dante, *The Divine Comedy, Paradiso*, Canto XXXI

Once upon a time, somewhere past a large field of low-growing spring soybeans, our traveller started to get the feeling he was lost.

In the middle of nowhere, I was looking for "the big gas station" where I was supposed to turn toward the town of McLouth, Kansas. Friends were anxiously awaiting my arrival at their new rented home in the country. "An old hippie house," they called it, "with a sauna." Unlike much of Kansas, the landscape in Jefferson County rolled with limestone bluffs lush with leafy elms, hackberry, redbud, and oak. If I hadn't known any better, I would have sworn I wasn't in Kansas anymore, that I'd entered a fable, a myth, some scene on a Grecian urn—*were these the dales of Arcady?* More than two hours on the road and seemingly lost, I wanted to click my heels, the way we Kansans can do, to be sure I could have made it back home. A humid breeze seemed almost to breathe, though we'd technically been in a drought for months. I knew what was to come in July, the spring-moist ground baked into an infernal earthenware, but then the thought seemed for the moment to have too much doom.

Country directions, I'd come to know, rarely specify roads by name. Instead, folks who actually live off these thinnest of map lines (if even on a map) prefer "the old road" or "the new road," "the corner where the church stands" or "the turnoff where the silo used to be." Nonetheless, I kept driving, looking for "the big gas station," while anticipating what was to come next at "find 24 Highway"—that's how they say it around here: number, then highway. There was no indication when I came to this crossroads that I should turn east or continue north, but when I arrived at 24 junction (admire my localese) and hadn't spotted "the big gas station," I turned, as I'm apt to do when given a choice between continuing down a familiar path or choosing a new one. Perhaps such turning is a metaphor for my life. I've never been much good at staying on one path for long. Maybe I'm a nomad of sorts, willed to roam the earth, something left over in the genes from my maternal grandparents, who fled Italy for a better chance at prosperity in America despite how they would be called dagos all their lives here. Or maybe this will to roam comes from the paternal side of my family; an old relative of mine had actually been a whaling-ship captain who regularly set sail from Salem, Massachusetts. "Never go straight," an old girlfriend used to tell me, a phrase having less to do with driving than it sounds. Though 24 Highway may not be the road less traveled, I was certain it would lead somewhere, perhaps to metaphor itself, the symbolic structure behind the literal journey, what the well-read read for, the pleasures of the text, if I may borrow the term, an accretion of moments that arrives at perception or the structural axis of tales like these.

In the distance a building appeared like a mirage on the wavering horizon. Its bright yellow marquee seemed a vision of sorts, like an oasis or an old roadside HoJo's. The closer I got, the more I felt I was headed the right direction, that this would finally be "the big gas station," a chance to stretch and buy a Slim Jim. Driving the 65-miles-per-hour speed limit, I found it difficult to read the distant sign and watch the road at the same time, something I failed to disclose in a recent driving examination for a license I'd unknowingly let expire. Lots of things in my life seemed to be expiring then: first my car needed tires, a drive belt, then an alternator; all of my teeth's fillings needed replacement and newer cavities needed fixing; my optometrist recommended a new prescription for my increasingly poor nearsightedness; home appliances were burning out faster than light bulbs; our once-overflowing pond had become a giant mud puddle; and my body moved like the rusted Sammy Davis, Jr., of his later years, the aftereffect of a grisly truck rollover I'd been in with my then-near-term pregnant wife (who some two weeks later gave birth to our lovely daughter—but that's not part of the story—then again, maybe it's everything).

Maybe these were life signs I should have been able to read like the blurry marquee. I was thirty-five going on thirty-six, the youngest male on a faculty of colleagues at my university who had years ago given up on the miracles of Grecian Formula 16 or the promises of Oil of Olay. I was closer to fifty than twenty, officially middle-aged though still "pretty cool," as some of my students liked to remind me, or as I flattered myself on occasion when buying new sunglasses or putting a dab of sports gel in my hair. I am, for the record, not contemplating a Steinach operation à la W. B. Yeats, a red Miata like the one my older brother from the "Me" generation purchased at the onset of middle age, nor do I need to succumb to fellow Kansan Bob Dole's sales pitch for a week's trial sample of Viagra, though I should be so lucky to need a week's supply. However, now in my middle years, I finally understand the metaphorical difference between Ravel's slowly building "Bolero" and a brief Eddie Van Halen guitar solo. I disclose the above laments not for pity, and, of course, I anticipate the "Get over it!" reader like my colleague Amy across the hall. I'm not writing for sympathy either because what happens next—and I say this only because the genre demands it—has very little to do with me and more to do with understanding why there is ubiquitous admiration for Keats's ever-popular, most-often-cited "Ode on a Grecian Urn," or Dante's enduring vision of Beatrice, the meanings of which had eluded me as a college freshman.

And so our lost traveller continued his journey toward the bright marquee.

Pulling into a gravel parking lot, I couldn't help but be struck by the towering sign above my vehicle's front bumper. I had found "Paradise," though under it were a few bold "X"s and "Live Nude Girls." Paradise was now only a few steps into a rectangular, cinder-brick building with little character. I parked my car on the end of a row of pickups with cold hoods, then contemplated my ethical dilemma: with no "big gas station" in sight, I could suck in my pride and go in to ask for directions or continue driving a road where I might never find the wizard or "the big gas station." So I decided, for the sake of my friends, of course, on directions.

The afternoon sun felt warm against my neck as I made my way to the entrance door with a mirrored porthole at eye level. Traffic not stopping at Paradise whizzed by along 24 Highway. Though I was technically, or perhaps metaphorically, in the middle of nowhere, I was strangely worried about who might see me enter the forbidden palace, this Bower of Bliss, as Spenser might have put it. Call it paranoia, in our day of easily concealed video cameras—Rob Lowe frolicking with teenagers,

Tonya Harding's wedding night, Pamela Anderson in heat with Tommy Lee—I worried about being taped entering a strip joint merely to ask directions. Would even my wife believe my innocence and naïveté?

I should confess here to the fact that up until that moment, I'd never so much as set a foot inside a strip joint, though I'd had my chances. Years ago, on my first-ever trip to Las Vegas, my buddies invited me to come along with them to the Palomino, a strip club we had spotted on our way into town. After driving all day through the canyons of Utah, the XXXs of the Palomino promised peeks and valleys of a different sort. Mesmerized as we were by the Vegas glow and neon, a night at the Palomino seemed the perfect introduction to our virgin tour of Sin City. To make a long story short, I had to opt out because I couldn't afford the cover charge (an odd name for a fee in a strip joint). I had crossed the entire country on some fifty dollars and had only a few left. While they went in without me, I walked the long blocks to the Strip, then parked my ass at a nickel slot where, trying to hit it big, I drank free beer until I assured myself of bed spins and a Nevada-style hangover. As my buddies, one the well-off son of a successful stockbroker and the other an avowed Deadhead son of a dentist, whooped it up at the Palomino, I was so destitute and drunk after losing all my money at the slots, I briefly contemplated mugging a Japanese tourist in the bathroom stall. Desperation, I learned, has a friend in criminal thoughts. Sometime about sunrise, I rendezvoused with my buddies at the now-demolished Jamaica Inn, a dive that had been about as glamorous as Kingston itself. What they had seen at the Palomino far surpassed anything I saw except for the legs of passing cocktail waitresses bringing me free beer.

My continued missed chances for "adult live entertainment," as it's often called in more polite parlance, have more to do with bad timing than any religious or moral matters. I care little about men or women who want to take off their clothes for money, attention, or to fulfill some exhibitionist desire—are nude people in a roadhouse in the middle of nowhere really that offensive or threatening? Are men just men? Are women who strip "demeaned, objectified, and exploited by the dominant patriarchy" as some of my colleagues might say? Or are they "empowered," as some third-wave feminists have put it, with control over their bodies and earning potential? And I won't bother to comment on religious or moral arguments that might involve a convoluted syntax, terms like hegemony and dominance, and/or some contradictory Puritan ideology. It seems, so long as there are people of either gender who want to see other people naked, and so long as people are willing to get naked for economic or other motivations, this debate will continue. And let's be honest, in purely economic terms, for the female or male dancer, the job is surely better than working the rendering line in a slaughterhouse. Perhaps if I'd had the body or the endowment, I might have considered nude dancing as an alternative to the demolition crew on which I'd once worked. The truth is, I have bad knees.

Our traveller prepared for what lay ahead.

   Gathering myself for what I might see when I walked into Paradise, I recited to myself a few lines of Dante, "O muse, O alto ingegno, or m'aiutate!" (O Muses, O high genius, now assist me!) Was I entering the Inferno's Second Circle for the "peccator carnali" (carnal sinners)? "Poeta che mi guidi, / guarda la mia virtù s'ell'è possente, / prima ch'a l'alto passo tu mi fidi." (Poet, who guidest me, / Regard my manhood, if it be sufficient, / Ere to the arduous pass thou dost confide me.)

   When I walked through the door into the foyer, I instantly detected the faint odor of some Kansas back-acre herb mixed with cigarettes, incense, and stale beer, something like my Deadhead friend's teenage bedroom. Inside the stuffy anteroom, the air was stale and warm, making me perspire a bit. I could pass through to the loud music only by paying the proper cover and showing a photo ID to a goon of a man, perhaps the Gorgon himself, sitting behind a Plexiglas window to my left. I assumed, given his simian stature and appearance, he was the bouncer. His black hair seemed jelled into place like cupcake icing or molded Jell-O, his biceps bulging from a T-shirt two sizes too small. Though a sizeable fellow, his baby face created a striking contrast, his skin dotted with patches of teenage acne.

Difficult to see much in the dim room, I took my wrinkled directions from my pocket, then presented them to him like a passport. "I'm looking for 'the big gas station,'" I shouted over the music. "Am I headed in the right direction?"

"Beats me," he said, looking at my crumpled paper.

"Is this still 24 Highway?"

"All the way to Tonganoxie."

"Been there before?" I asked.

"Never," he said. "But it's about ten miles up the road," he told me with the confidence of having made the drive for years.

Over his shoulder, I could see the stage with a wall of mirrors behind it. However, the view from the lobby, if lobby it could be called, only permitted me to see dancing legs multiplied by the mirrors into a harem. I wiped away the sweat on my forehead and tried to stay focused on the bouncer, though my eyes drifted to the legs when they passed, glowing in the soft spotlight. Such legs made me want to crane my neck into a position that would have been most embarrassing for an innocent man seeking only directions. Below the stage, I could see a scattering of the backs of men's heads separated from one another by the darkness. I wondered if they were drawn here on a hot afternoon by something hormonal or primal, by an infernal lust of sorts, by something sexually deviant, or perhaps as a way to forget their plain lives or aging libidos. Maybe some came to appreciate the female body, which these days, except perhaps for those enrolled in a studio art class, might seem criminal to confess in certain circles. Maybe none of the above. Maybe all of the above. *Who are these coming to the sacrifice?*

The music thumped so loudly, I could barely hear the bouncer when he attempted to say something to me as I watched the legs pass again. As the feet in stiletto heels moved in time with the music and multiplied in the mirror, a slight gyration hijacked my midriff, luring me further into Paradise, to the songs of sirens in the wan light.

"Can't help, pal, I'm new around here," the bouncer shouted again, disrupting my vision and loud enough for me to understand he meant "pay up or get out."

I wanted to ask him what would make a man take a job at a strip joint in the middle of nowhere—then again, the answer seemed obvious enough. I assume, generalizing on appearance, that he wasn't an honors student at the university in Lawrence, though it crossed my mind that perhaps he was on a football scholarship or on parole. For a moment, as the shapely legs passed again, I contemplated requesting of him momentary entry so as I could ask the bartender for directions to "the big gas station." I did, that is, until I realized how ridiculous and desperate it would sound to a goon familiar with just about every ploy from horny men seeking free entry to this garden. Despite his youthful face, he struck me as an experienced bouncer, a man with bulging biceps accustomed to throwing short fellows like me out of front doors. About the moment I realized all of this, he left his booth to escort me out the door. "Really, pal," he said, pushing open the door to a light that nearly blinded me, "it's not a long drive."

Outside, the sun seemed much brighter and hotter than our traveller remembered.

Among all the pickups, I had no problem finding my car, a Chevy Lumina family sedan with A/C, security locks, and cruise control, a stark contrast to the cowboy cruisers. The salesman had claimed my A/C could blow frost in the desert. "But I don't live in a desert," I told him deadpan, though he assured me, if I ever drove in the desert anytime soon, the Lumina would handle it with ease. A/C or no A/C, I bought the car not because of any sales pitch but because *Consumer Reports* gave it a high safety rating, much higher, I will add, than for my 4x4 S-10 Chevy Blazer that rolled like a sea otter after being struck from behind, the roof collapsing in on itself. I like to think I survived my crash fairly well considering what could have happened had I been a tall man or had my seat belt not held. From the accident, I only have recurring nightmares, a sense that absurdity and chance are the most basic laws of our universe, a chronic back problem that feels like a rusty hinge between my tailbone and lumbar that throbs with pain after long sittings and after certain hip movements I can't discuss here, and an extreme paranoia about tailgaters.

As I griped to myself about my sore back, the frosty A/C began to blow over me. After Paradise and no new clue as to the whereabouts of "the big gas station," I felt as if I were in a purgatory of sorts, neither here nor there, just short of halfway from the middle of nowhere. I was thinking about giving up my trip to see my friends at their hippie home with a sauna. Despite their invitation, I figured they probably didn't need somebody like me hanging around anyway. Young couples can dream up plenty to do to keep themselves busy.

While I contemplated my near future, the bouncer came out to check the perimeter. I waved to him, but he didn't wave back. I went over my choices again: find "the big gas station" or head back into the club to experience Paradise as fully as Hugh Hefner would recommend (what's not to admire in the symbolism of the accomplished capitalist, a martini-drinking man who spends all day in silk pajamas surrounded by beautiful women?). I thought about all my missed chances, how I've tried almost everything legal and illegal once in my life, and the things I've enjoyed at least twice. Luckily, every time the subject of nudie bars had come up among friends, male or female, I'd somehow been able to avoid a confession, as if masking my virginity in a high school locker room. I thought again about the passing legs, the lights and sirens, the music's boom-boom until I felt it was almost my American duty, a duty performed daily and nightly by our brave seamen in ports worldwide, to walk back into Paradise, a literary obligation to you, the readers, that only Robert Herrick (Oh how that glittering taketh me!), Henry Miller, or Anaïs Nin would properly understand. *A thing of beauty is a joy forever.*

II.

però che 'l ben, ch'è del volere obietto,
tutto s'accoglie in lei, e fuor di quella
è defettivo ciò ch'è lì perfetto.

Because the good, which object is of will,
Is gathered all in this, and out of it
That is defective which is perfect there.

—Dante, *The Divine Comedy, Paradiso,* Canto XXXIII

Once again, fate had barred our traveller from the fierce Erinyes and the City of Dis.

As my Lumina glided over the gentle hills of Jefferson County, I felt as if I had entered another world, perhaps one painted on a Grecian urn. The land seemed greener than earlier, as elm and hackberry swayed in the warm wind. It was as if a vortex had carried me from black and white to Technicolor, an exuberance glittering from the hillsides and in the newly sprouting fields. I cut the A/C, then rolled down my windows to let the air thick with moisture wash over me, as if to envelop myself in the very spirit of spring. If I were in some kind of myth or pastoral, then I wanted to feel like it. The scene was so delightful, I half expected at any moment the day's narrative to pause so I could break into song, the way it happens in musicals. Instead of taking 24 Highway further toward Tonganoxie, I had decided to turn back toward the last crossroads I'd passed on the chance that I'd missed "the big gas station," an assumption that proved correct. On second glance, the station I found seemed grossly misnamed by my friends who provided the directions; perhaps "two-story gas station" or "antique gas station" would have been more appropriate, as the white, two-floored wooden building resembled an old roadhouse where travelers might have been given dinner and a bed, or perhaps, for an additional charge, some evening company. I also figured that, to people living in the country, any gas station in the middle of nowhere would seem bigger than nothing, so I was inclined to forgive.

At "the two-story gas station" I turned onto Douglas County 1045, which had no dividing line. While 55 miles per hour seemed to be pushing the limit on this thin stretch of aging blacktop, I was expected to drive 65 or get bumped into the drainage ditch by a speeding hick driving a used pickup he'd be paying off for the next decade. Despite the rather high speed limit and my affinity for Sammy Hagar, 55 was all I had the courage to go. Every so often, as the road rose and fell over sloping hills, a truck going 70 passed with hardly a swish on my left. I again began searching for landmarks, a field where I needed to turn toward Lake Dabinawa (which sounded to me like a summer camp in the Catskills), a stop sign at Union Street (a dirt crossroad in the middle of nowhere that I was amazed had a name), Skip and Fran's bridge (noticeable after passing Skip and Fran's mailbox), then a right at the next drive, down into a gulch that would lead back up to where I was supposed to honk just in case anybody else was coming along the one-way drive.

As I pulled into a field of tall grass, I saw for the first time my friends' hippie house, a round glass structure at the edge of a wooded ravine, perhaps something paradisal. Constructed from cement, fieldstone, glass, and oddly cut boards, the structure would by no means pass county housing codes. For that matter then, it was an outlaw's shack of sorts, on the margins of society, which would make Thoreau proud. The round structure reached about three stories high and twenty feet in diameter with windows on all sides and a wild beehive on top. It resembled a glass tree house more than anything. Dogwood and redbud surrounded their wooden deck off the entrance some ten feet above ground, accessible by a flight of stairs. From the deck, there was a panoramic view of the field and garden where, on the edge, sat a small outbuilding or shed which, I would find out later, was their sauna.

Sitting on the deck, where they waved and smiled to me as I got out of the car, were my young friends, Mr. Tecate Man, a beer already in hand, and his girlfriend, Red. I presented them with a couple of six-packs of Tecate for old times' sake.

"I take it you had no problem with my directions," he said. "In the future you might try 'two-story gas station.'"

"It's really pretty big. Don't you think?" he returned.

"Bigger than most," Red added.

"Everything's relative," I told them. "But I found Paradise."

"That's where all the rednecks hang out," said Mr. Tecate Man.

"I didn't see too many necks," I told him.

"There's a story how at one of these places William Burroughs once showed up with Iggy Pop. I think it's mostly a tall tale."

"Whatever happened to Dennis Hopper in Taos?" I asked.

"What?"

"Never mind."

"Let me show you around," Red said, getting out of her patio chair to greet me. Red grew up in the Solomon River valley in the north central part of the state. When I first met her during her sophomore year at my college, she had stunning long red hair halfway down her back, though at some point during my Poetry Writing class, for reasons she never disclosed, she cropped it at her neckline. She's also not too fond of me calling her Red in these pages. "Too stereotypical," she told me, "something I had to hear all my life." When I threatened to use Wilma for her because I thought pop-culture buff Mr. Tecate Man would have appreciated a partner named Wilma (who also has red hair in *The Flintstones*), she reluctantly reconsidered. If I may say so, like Mr. Tecate Man, Red's a good writer, that rare student who actually embraced the challenges of learning. She was not afraid to take chances on the page, nor, it seemed, in choosing to live in a remote glass tree house with Mr. Tecate Man. My bet is that she can even skin a catfish. That's not to say she doesn't have a delicate and caring side; I had trusted her for most of a semester to look after my infant daughter.

So our traveller pondered over the strange house and his frolicsome friends.

Tour guide Red led me down a spiraling flight of stairs into their tiny kitchen somewhat below ground level. Compared to the rest of the place, we were low enough to see tree trunks and the grasshoppers jumping in the weeds outside the recessed window. The smell of late spring was everywhere present in the colonies of mold and mildew. The dim room with its stone floor seemed carved out of the earth like a cave. I could feel the humidity pressing itself through the walls, which gave me the sneaking suspicion that they had moved into the tree house in good weather, when there was little need for insulation. I was amazed they had running water and electricity. "The gas is propane," she told me. During the winter, on a day far less dreamy and temperate, Mr. Tecate Man would call me from a Motel 6 to say how their pipes had frozen and how it would be some time before a repairman could make the drive on snowy back roads to fix them. On this dreamy day, however, the summer's short lease seemed to matter little, if at all.

The tour continued from the cellar up a spiral staircase to a small sitting room, then up again another level to their bedroom. With its uneven floors and many steps, the tree house seemed built for a young couple. With floor-to-ceiling windows and views of the woods, their bedroom was truly lovely. "If you listen closely, you can hear the bees," Red told me, and I could, a droning hum coming from the ceiling. Large dogwood leaves pressed against the windows, almost as if they could reach their wide bed taking up most of the room's space like a raft in a sea of trees and light. I imagined how each morning they woke to the dawn harmonies of birds, how each night in the middle of nowhere the darkness seemed pure, how the sky overflowed with stars. "I bet you get used to rising early or learn how to sleep in a bright room," I told her.

"Not me," Red added, though I refused to amend the quaint picture I had imagined. A late-afternoon sun filtered through the crisscrossed vines that hung from elm branches—*We're not in Kansas anymore*, I thought. The whole time I climbed up and down their many stairs, I couldn't help but think they were living in an Oz of their own making. Plainly, I was envious.

One level below their magical bedroom was the sitting room I'd passed on my way to the upper floor. There was only a small black-and-white TV along with Mr. Tecate Man's vast collection of tapes, CDs, and albums, from Brazilian Gilberto Gil to Mexican-American *corridos* by Américo Paredes. Here Red told me that the outbuilding next to their garden was the sauna. "Perhaps we can all go for a steam," she suggested without the slightest bit of innuendo. Because they were my friends and former students, I tried not to imagine their sweaty bodies merrymaking in the warmth or how, dripping with moisture, they might chase each other up the many winding stairs to their bedroom, all the sex that must go on when you have lots of time together with a sauna, some beer, and good music.

After listening to some of their newer CDs, music I hardly recognized, Red and I made our way out to their deck. She told me how they spent their days writing poems, working in their vegetable garden, snoozing in the afternoon, and stargazing at night. Then I felt a bit out of place and out of my time. Years ago (cue the shaggy-dog music), I'd led a similar carefree life with a live-in girlfriend (now my wife) in a beach house in Del Mar, California, where I worked on my first failed book, smoked too much reefer, and surfed away my afternoons. Back then, the only thing I cared about, outside my dream to publish a successful book of poems, was how to come up with money for beer. I worked odd jobs or painted houses until I got paid, then didn't work again until I ran out of money. I was sure then there was more to life than good insurance and a regular paycheck, and I took for granted how easy it was to drive out to the Anza Borrego desert with two sleeping bags and a cooler of beer because we wanted to learn the constellations.

Below us, Mr. Tecate Man swatted away bees as he tried to get his barbecue started in a dead calm. Soon, down yet another flight of stairs, we gathered around him, watched as he hopelessly fanned at the coals with an old album, *He Touched Me* by Cliff Johnson, which he said he bought only for the irony: the first two songs were, respectively, "He Touched Me" and "Then Jesus Came," followed by "I've Found a Friend" and "In the Garden"—*now what was this guy's last name?*

After giving up, Mr. Tecate Man tossed the album to me, where on the back I noticed that Cliff had autographed and dated the cover, "2-2-75 Celebration of Faith Weekend." On the front, a balding, middle-aged man I assumed to be Cliff rested his elbows on a red tabletop and held a cup of joe in his hands as if in prayer. A blurb on the cover, which I read out loud, offered the tale of Cliff's inspiration: "My mind went back over the years of failure as a father.... There in the quiet of our kitchen, I reached out in faith.... He touched me right there and then and made a new person of me."

"How's that for a story?" asked Mr. Tecate Man. "You'll never think of your kitchen in the same way again."

"Inspiring," I told him. "There's still hope for each of us. If it happened tonight, we could call it 'The Barbecue Conversion.'"

"Now that's hot," he punned and we all laughed.

All joking aside, what wasn't so funny was how I'd come, like Cliff, to believe that epiphanies large and small can happen anywhere. I'd had them, like teenage sex, almost everywhere except in a tree house or in my kitchen (what goes on in my kitchen, be assured, is nothing like that scene from *9 1/2 Weeks*). And, in Cliff's defense, it just seemed right that an epiphany of such magnitude should be accompanied by something like a hot cup of joe, a good meal, slice of pie, bar of chocolate, bowl of ice cream, or a cold beer. Then I realized I'd just had an epiphany about epiphanies while thinking of epiphanies, in other words, a meta-epiphany (jargon that would impress my colleagues who call themselves literary theorists). As I looked at the smoldering coals, a word surfaced in my head, not *Rosebud* but *Fusion*, a simple word that would bind together this day:

Fusion
    3.c. *(i) Psychol.* and *Physiol.* [tr. G. *Verschmelzung* (J. F. Herbert *Psychol. als Wiss.* (1824) *I.* 200).] A blending together of separate simultaneous sensations into a new complex experience or qualitative perception; the process whereby a succession of similar stimuli produces a continuous response or the sensation of a continuous stimulus ...
    (ii) Psychiatry. [tr. G. *Mischung* (Freud *Das Ich und das Es* (1923) *IV.* 50).] In Freudian theory, the union and balance of life and death instincts which exist in normal persons. (*OED*)

I turned to the glass house that towered before me. *Verschmelzung und Mischung, Verschmelzung und Mischung,* I chanted like a spell. From the day's various stimuli, those parts of a larger metaphor, emerged a complex experience, an ode of sorts on beauty and art, youth and age, Byzantium.

I looked hard at the glass structure. Despite the home's many flaws and uneven floors that questioned the very notions of balance and stability, the tree house appeared a truly beautiful and inspiring idea from a time not long ago that wanted to believe in love, peace, and Bobby Dylan, even during a war. I knew there is a brief time in all of our lives when we desire to live in a tree house somewhere close to the sky and stars. Icarus House, I wanted to name it, where imagination takes fight, where the ambitious boy cannot be permitted to become his father. *But at my back I always hear / Time's wingèd chariot hurrying near,* I wanted to recite for my friends, but they wouldn't have understood. I thought about that darkness inside Paradise as well, how it saved men in the audience from looking too hard at themselves, at what surrounded them, or at what awaited them outside. As with a midsummer comedy or Grecian urn, what matters is a dream of agelessness, its mad pursuit and wild ecstasy, *For ever wilt thou love, and she be fair!*

As the warm afternoon became a muggy evening, as frogs began to sing from damp ravines, I drank and ate with ease. The hamburgers seemed to taste better than usual, the strawberries we had for dessert somehow sweeter. After dinner, we toured their sprouting garden—green beans, zucchini, spinach, basil, tomatoes, cayenne peppers, bell peppers, and cucumbers. Red told me with enthusiasm how in the coming weeks they would no longer need to drive into town for groceries, how not having jobs would be less of a burden with fewer things to buy. *O Attic shape!* I didn't have the heart to tell her otherwise; in Kansas, with thundershowers that can flatten crops in seconds, tornadoes that can blow them away, or heat that can wither them in an afternoon—not to mention drought, grasshoppers, aphids, rabbits, and deer—a young gardener needs such optimism.

Thinking back, I like to believe I've captured in these pages something special about my friends and their tree house life—

Verschmelzung und Mischung. However, I must confess to feeling I've created here more of an idyll. With this in mind, permit me the right ending, a touch of artifice with a hint of Keats that will make sense to my friends at forty or perhaps some six months hence, on that wind-chilled day in their dim room at the Motel 6.

Later that evening, after claiming I was too tired to join them for a sauna, I caught Red looking at Mr. Tecate Man and he at her in a way that seemed to forget I would be lying for the night in the middle of their floor. After more music and a few more drinks, I stretched out on a blanket in their sitting room hoping the mellow incantations of Gilberto Gil would lull me to sleep. I was certain those soothing Brazilian rhythms would make for good dancing or a sensuous massage. The steamy spring humidity and frolicsome laughter coming from the sauna were keeping me awake despite the drink. I felt the season's evanescence. *É defettivo ciò ch'è lì perfetto,* I thought, *O quanto è corto il dire e come fioco / al mio concetto!* (That is defective which is perfect there ... O how all speech is feeble and falls short / Of my conceit!) I let my muse wander out the glass windows, past the trees and dewy grass where the crickets and frogs were still going strong—*O love, O Careless Love, Come out! Come out!* they seemed to sing, *All ye need to know.* Looking at the innumerable stars glinting above the garden, I let my self drift up.

GO, GO, GO

Their sons grow suicidally beautiful
At the beginning of October,
And gallop terribly against each other's bodies.

—James Wright
"Autumn Begins in Martins Ferry, Ohio"

Football is a way of life. Really. It really is.... I think that
football is the symbol, really, of a lot of things.

—Vince Lombardi
"Dinner Conversation with Vince Lombardi"

Everywhere I travel, I take along a ham sandwich, three ibuprofens, two Rolaids, and one large vitamin C caplet. At 6:45 a.m. in Norman, Oklahoma, it was no different, though I'd resisted taking the ibuprofen after a relatively sleepless night. Regardless of how I felt, I knew I looked good, a brown plaid jacket, crisp white shirt, and a pair of pressed Levi's. In the lobby of the Hampton Inn, I'd left behind a packed room full of red-shirted Husker fans from Lincoln, Nebraska, who, smelling like stale beer and coffee, were stuffing themselves as well as their pockets with sweet rolls from the free continental breakfast. Outside, not wanting to soil my maintenance-free

Florsheims, I avoided large puddles of standing water from a late-night October thunderstorm while I searched for my car sandwiched between two Nebraska RVs, each larger than the square footage of my Kansas apartment. Flying low, a small plane stuttered along, pulling a banner across Norman, "Bob's BBQ, Do the Q," which made me wonder how many people order a slab of ribs for breakfast.

There were five hours to go before the big game, Sooners versus Huskers, for the country's number-one ranking in the 2000 season, although I was in Norman for another reason. A poet of sorts, I was up before my muse in order to make it on time to a reading I was supposed to give shortly after the noon hour, some six hours later, at an event billed enthusiastically as the "Vistas of the Word" in conjunction with the Western Literature Association (for some reason I kept calling the event a more self-flattering "Vistas of the World," but it was early). Under normal circumstances, the drive from the Hampton Inn to the University of Oklahoma's conference center is a routine fifteen minutes at best, something I could easily have covered after a quick lunch at a nearby oyster bar (and I'm not talking the Rocky Mountain kind), but this was no normal day for an unheard-of poet like myself. It was a Saturday during football season, and, clearly, whoever scheduled the conference at the center, within a block of the stadium, was not a football fan. As serendipity would have it, this was also the weekend that the Sooners, back from a fifteen-year drought, were once again contenders for the top ranking. If the Huskers' five national championships seemed daunting, OU's Sooners on this very weekend began their quest for number seven, but first they would need to get past the Big Red defense, flush the Nebraska quarterback from the pocket, commandeer their own offensive arsenal, and create holes for their running game—what did I know of football?

My situation could have been easily averted had I not attempted to make last-minute reservations at the conference center's student-run hotel, the Sooner Inn. As history would have it, Oklahoma is no state for latecomers. My good friend and fellow reader, Peter Donahue, a former resident of Norman and author of the collection of stories *The Cornelius Arms*, had tried to warn me of the possible take-what-you-can-find scenario. He booked his room months in advance. Even Hugh Tribbey, a professor of English at East Central University in Ada, Oklahoma, and coordinator of the "Vistas" reading, had advised me about booking early, no abstract idea indeed. Because I had failed to heed the oracle's warning, I was lucky to end up across town at the Hampton Inn after having tried ten or more sold-out hotels, including a handful I turned down because of the jacked-up rates. Perhaps Fortune had shined her light upon me when I found the only reasonably priced available room in Norman, complete with a queen bed, faux cherry armoire, cable TV with thirteen static-free channels (at home, I have two relatively clear channels, CBS and FOX, although I get ABC and PBS if the wind is right), and a continental breakfast that included biscuits and gravy, Quaker Instant Oatmeal, Kellogg's Corn Flakes, Post Raisin Bran, sweet rolls and Danishes, cream cheese and bagels, coffee, tea, orange juice, and milk (whole and skim).

At 6:45 a.m., besides the traffic and my early backache that would only worsen, I'd lucked out. Just outside the Hampton was a comforting plethora of highway chains, from Applebees to the Olive Garden. Norman's Fashion Square Mall was also within walking distance, which was extremely lucky as my wife and baby girl had come down with me for the shopping and dining. While I'm not complaining, Norman could have been even more welcoming had it been possible to eradicate the hordes of Husker fans creating long restaurant waits, traffic jams, and plenty of noise as they stomped up and down the Hampton's halls arriving throughout the night liquored up and with plenty of esprit de corps. Nonetheless, Norman seemed like a culinary paradise of the highest order compared to where we live in Emporia, Kansas, with our Super Wal-Mart (its food court always packed with chain-smoking truckers, farmers, and the hopelessly unemployed) two Burger Kings, two Wendy's, two McDonald's (three Mickey D's if you count the one on the turnpike seven miles north), two Dairy Queens, two Hardee's, two Subways, two Braum's, two Taco Bells, a Taco Tico, Mr. Goodcents, Long John Silver's, Arby's, KFC, Domino's Pizza, Mazzio's Pizza, Gambino's Pizza, Godfather's Pizza, and a Pyramid Pizza (local chain) to serve our population of roughly twenty-five thousand, not officially counting the migrant workers at the beef plant who represent a whopping 20 to 25 percent silent minority.

As I inched off the Ed Nobel Parkway onto Lindsey Street, which would take me to the campus, I couldn't help but remember the morning's ride down the elevator from my second-floor room, an elevator I had shared with two Husker-sized men, their Husker-sized wives, and their two Husker-sized coolers with Husker bumper stickers, everything red from their ice chests to the wives' hair ribbons, including their shoes. I should have taken the ride as another sign of things to come, but I'm an optimist by nature, and was still certain that the day would turn out all right despite the football hoopla I had yet to fully understand. "I'm a poet of sorts in town for a reading," I wanted to tell them, but it had seemed too early for me to be friendly or to welcome the typical "I write poems, too" refrain. The smell of beer was fresh on their breath, as if they had gargled with Miller Lite upon waking. A teetotaler I am not, and if asked, I would have probably joined them for a cold one to clear my head and soothe my back pain on our short ride down to the lobby. Back in college, my roommate and I used to drink Saturday morning pick-me-ups just to forget the sting from the night before. Though these fans looked a good number of years out of college, they still honored that oldest of collegiate morning traditions.

Three miles from Memorial Stadium's Owen Field, which could have been three thousand, people placed signs in their yards for five-dollar parking, a fair deal by national parking standards that can run as high as ten to twelve dollars on game days. While at this early hour there were still spaces available, most of these amateur parking attendants appeared quite confident that, by game time, every last space, including those in front yards, backyards, and fire lanes, would be filled. At not quite 7:00 a.m., packs of frat boys, most of who probably never heard of Bennie Owen, wandered the street toward the stadium. Along the sidewalk, folks had already begun to barbecue, the smoke wafting over their lawn chairs toward my car, raising in me a hunger for hot wings not satiated in years. Only my need to arrive at the conference center before the police closed down the street mitigated my desire to pull over to join the party and devour a paper plate stacked high with wings. From the looks of things, I knew it was going to be one hell of a blast, perhaps the best party I'd been at since the festivities in the parking lot before Dead shows years ago. While my reading, a half hour more or less of linguistic *tai chi chuan*, would certainly release in my limited audience a *jouissance* of sorts no fan of the pigskin could ever understand, it would never compare to the spectacle taking shape around me.

If I had had the cash and if the crimson-colored OU T-shirts for sale from curbside vendors didn't clash with my brown blazer, I might have bought one to wear at my reading. For a moment, I thought about pulling over to sell copies of my book out of my trunk, "Poems, get your poems here!" If asked, I would have signed the books, too. "To my friends in Norman, best fans in all the world!" or, if necessary, "To my friends from Lincoln, best fans in all the world!" Then it hit me, perhaps somewhere between a group grilling burgers and another turning sausage, that this game, red-shirted versus their crimson-shirted rivals, would be a nightmare for the color blind.

To assuage my irritability in the slow-going traffic, I downed three ibuprofens sans water, as only real men with significant back problems can, then chewed two Rolaids to kill the expected acid reflux. To keep my mind off my reading, I tried to count those already eating hot dogs, my morning oatmeal and two large cups of free, industrial-strength Hampton coffee less than an hour in my stomach with the just-swallowed ibuprofen and Rolaids. I tried as well to recall if I'd ever eaten a hot dog before 7:00 a.m., though I felt certain I must have, especially on one of the many Boy Scout camp-outs I went on as a kid. Before my wheels began to roll again, I counted an easy five wiener eaters, not figuring what appeared to be a similar number of burger munchers. Then I realized that if just five thousand people in the stadium's vicinity ate two hot dogs in an hour that would amount to roughly ten thousand hot dogs consumed before 8:00 a.m.; if repeated each hour by a similar number of newcomers, a staggering forty thousand could be consumed by kickoff, with eight dogs to the pound, that would be roughly five thousand pounds. If all 75,004 in the stadium, not including vendors, janitorial staff, and security, ate just one dog, that would come to about 9,375.5 pounds, a number of truly superlative proportions. Despite ingredients that included pork by-products (heads to tails), sodium caseinate, potassium chloride, sodium phosphates, sodium erythrobate, oleoresin paprika, sodium nitrate, and "flavor," the numbers for hot dogs alone was monumental, not counting hamburgers, bratwurst, or those chicken wings that folks consume by the stack. Similar numbers could be arrived at for beer and wine consumption. However, if people spent hours eating and drinking, they would eventually need a parking lot full of Porta-Potties, which is exactly what I found on campus, the potties strategically placed about so as to seem as unobtrusive as Coke machines. The game, I slowly came to understand, was much more than white lines placed ten yards apart on green grass.

A bit further up the road, past yard signs exclaiming "Bob Stoops for President" that would make Tom Osborne envious, I would get my first sighting of Memorial Stadium, which would rise in size and grandeur the closer I came. Named after Coach

Bennie Owen, the OU stadium, at its 75,004 capacity, can seat three quarters of the population of Norman, but sadly it's only the nineteenth largest college stadium in the country. However, if size matters, by comparison the Huskers' Memorial Stadium, which has sold out continuously since 1962, can seat a mere 74,031, though there'd be enough room for everybody in Lincoln plus friends. While I'm no aficionado of stadiums, I will admit to feeling a bit giddy upon first sighting the OU structure, as if I, too, were going to the game and not giving a poetry reading. It's an excitement I felt as a child when nearing Chicago's Soldier Field on a subzero Sunday morning, or perhaps that first time I glimpsed the Roman Colosseum or the original Greek Olympic grounds. It's a euphoria similar to what my father-in-law must have felt when he himself first sighted the OU stadium with me a few years back.

Although my father-in-law is somebody whom I might consider a near-native Californian, having lived in the Los Angeles area most of his life, he was born in Tulsa, Oklahoma, and lived there until he was about seven. As was fashionable for many Okies, his family went west in search of greater fortune; however, they always remained true to their Okie roots, or "ruts," preserving a love to "warsh" clothes and a loyalty to OU football. These early years for my father-in-law coincided with the legendary Bud Wilkinson era, a seventeen-year tenure that resulted in three national championships ('50, '56, '57) and a 1952 Heisman trophy–winner (halfback Billy Vessels from Cleveland, Oklahoma). To somebody like my father-in-law, who for years had harbored a love both for the Sooners and for college football more generally, the chance to visit Owen Field must have been a dream come true.

To make a long story short, I had provided for him that once-in-a-lifetime opportunity when I decided to move back to the Middle West for graduate school after a brief and expensive stint of living on the West Coast. Upon deciding to return and after I convinced my then-bride-to-be of the better life in reverse migration, her father offered to help us with the move, as long as we took a detour to Norman, Oklahoma, to see the field. As my father-in-law is a man who lives religiously for football, especially college football, it was a chance of a lifetime for him. In the days before our trip, his enthusiasm grew larger than his big-screen television with its one hundred and fifty satellite stations, most of them sports channels. I'll confess now to secretly mocking his desire to see the stadium, and more so as we drove on a blistering day across Oklahoma toward Norman. The shallow man I was, I had yet to come to a full realization of and appreciation for what OU football means to Okies, and, more generally, what football itself means to others from the Plains states and beyond. While I had been on a homecoming trip back to familiar Middle Western ground, my father-in-law was on a pilgrimage satisfying a desire in him akin to my own to see the Ralph Waldo Emerson home in Concord, Massachusetts.

With distinct clarity, I can still recall that 100-plus-degree day when we turned off Interstate 40 (which replaced the old Route 66 traveled decades earlier by my father-in-law's parents) onto I-35 south en route to Norman and the Stadium. The night before, at a diner in Albuquerque, my father-in-law was already full of excitement, proudly telling us of OU's great football history, including the scandalous but victorious Barry Switzer years. For sixteen years, Switzer led OU, like Wilkinson, to three national championships ('74, '75, '85). On the way, OU became the first team ever to win back-to-back championships twice, and added Heisman-winner number three, Billy Simms (1978) from Hooks, Texas, to a list that already included Vessels (1952) and Steve Owens (1969) from Miami, Oklahoma (Jason White would be added to the list in 2003). With such an illustrious history, it's hard to remember that Troy Aikman, UCLA star and three-time Super Bowl quarterback (XXVII, XXVIII, XXX), broke his leg starting for OU in their '85 national championship season, a position filled by the heroics of Jamelle Hollieway on an outstanding '85 pigskin honor roll that also included Tony

Casillas, Brian Bosworth (subsequently dismissed by Switzer), and Keith Jackson. Everybody needs heroes.

As the hot road wavered ahead of us late the following afternoon, we drove into Norman, everything I owned piled into the back of my Ford Escort and all that my wife cherished, besides me, of course, in the back of her Buick Skyhawk driven by her parents. Though later that night, somewhere outside Tulsa, her old Buick's battery would fry out from the day's heat, we had managed not only to see but to walk on the hallowed football grounds, then a superheated, spongy Super Turf. At the moment his feet touched the carpet, my father-in-law seemed to tear up, a moment of unbridled sentiment and awe not witnessed again until the arrival of his granddaughter a decade later.

Nearing pigskin Mecca for the second time in my life, I should have felt blessed. Like many Americans, much of my life has revolved directly or indirectly around football. I received my first significant bloody nose sometime around the first grade while playing tackle with my older brother's junior-high friends. Then there were those Bear games at Soldier Field that I attended annually with my father and his season-ticket-holding stockbroker, a man who would later sell me an unfortunate number of shares of the now-bankrupt Borden Chemicals and Plastics. These were hard times for Chicago sports fans, before Walter Payton, Jim McMahon, and William "the Fridge" Perry, when the Bears couldn't give away enough seats to guarantee the game would be televised. Looking back, I should have enjoyed more those precious moments of itchy long underwear and frozen toes, as it's not often a boy gets to see beer dumped on his father in subzero weather by a drunk, whom my old man gallantly restrained himself from punching. Then, if memory serves me right, there are football-related stories concerning my father's bridge-playing, squirrel-shooting buddy, who, for some unaccountable reason perhaps having to do with his divorce, stored his old college equipment in our basement. What I remember most about this equipment was its sheer size, a huge leather helmet and pants so gigantic that my brother and I could each stand in a leg (it's not hard to believe this man could eat an entire duck for breakfast, or so the story goes).

As long as I'm citing personal football lore, I should also include my one and only trip to Notre Dame Stadium with my neighbor, Flaky Blake (nicknamed after his abnormally dry skin), where we saw a future Hall-of-Famer Joe Montana lose a game in the fourth quarter, despite the blessings of the Touchdown Jesus of the Hesburgh Library mural. In subsequent years, even though a love for Notre Dame football never took root within me, I'd come to watch countless times, purely for its kitschy appeal, *Knute Rockne—All American* (1940), starring Ronald Reagan as George Gipp, the player who died of pneumonia, and Pat O'Brien as Knute Rockne, the coach who uttered to his team those inspiring words, "Win just one for the Gipper." And, while I'm tempted to believe in bizarre correspondences between my life and those of football legends, it's surely a coincidence that, in a Flint Hills field less than thirty miles from my front door, near the cattle station ghost town of Bazaar, Knute Rockne met an untimely and gruesome death on March 31, 1931, in a TWA crash of a Fokker F-10A Trimotor flying in foggy weather.

At the start of high school, I would have another brush with the life of a football legend. I began my first afternoon as a freshman at the Jesuit-run Loyola Academy in Wilmette, Illinois (which comedian Bill Murray also once attended), with a mandatory viewing of a Vince Lombardi documentary. Yogi Berra of the gridiron, father of the motivational maxim, and winner of five world championships ('61, '62, '65, '66, '67), Lombardi is famous for saying things I once believed my father made up himself, typically when bouncing quarters off our beds during morning room inspections before school, on our way to and from church, or at the family dinner table. Soak in the wisdom of Lombardi, an American perhaps quoted more often than Ben Franklin or Knute Rockne:

"It's not whether you get knocked down, it's whether you get up."

"They may not love you at the time, but they will later."

"You've got to win the war with the man in front of you. You've got to get your man."

"Football is a great deal like life in that it teaches that work, sacrifice, perseverance, competitive drive, selflessness, and respect for authority is the price each and every one of us must pay to achieve any goal that is worthwhile."

Though the Lombardi film seemed to mesmerize almost every student in the theater, I suffered a laugh attack in the back row minutes after sharing a joint in the boys' bathroom with a buddy of mine called Fumes (for obvious reasons). I should have taken the incident as a sign that the priestly vocation would not call upon me no matter how much I prayed each night and no matter how hard I tried to refrain from extracurricular activities with Marilac girls in the parking lot during the fortnightly Friday-night home games. Perhaps, however, these games were responsible for the genesis of my muse. Not long after, I began to write love verse in the pages of my algebra notebook during Mr. Sirpy's first-period class. Then again, perhaps I was the kind of person Vince Lombardi had in mind when he said: "The values of duty and respect for authority must be embraced ... I am sure you are disturbed like I am of what seems to be a complete breakdown of law and order and the moral code which is almost beyond belief." It would take me even longer to realize how cheated we were at the University of California, San Diego, which I attended in the mid-eighties, by not having a football team or campus fraternities during those years. I wouldn't understand what I had missed out on until I moved to Manhattan, Kansas, "the Little Apple," to pursue a master's degree at Kansas State, though that was years before the Wildcat resurgence, player crime, the new highway to town from the interstate, the new campus fitness center, the new art museum, the new library, and the big stadium addition. All things considered, perhaps it wasn't until that fateful day in Norman, my second chance to stand before Owen Field, that I truly grasped any of the sport's cultural imperative.

As I reached the guarded perimeter outside the stadium sometime about 7:30 a.m., I was already a few bites into the ham sandwich I'd brought along for lunch. After all that time in my car, I'd developed a strong taste for ham, not to mention chicken wings and hot dogs, despite their ingredients. Nearing a wall of concrete barriers, I was quickly stopped by R. Williams, one of the OU campus policemen: "Where to?" he asked.

"The Vistas of the Word readings," I told him. If I were willing to press my luck, I might have said that I was a poet, too, one of the event's featured writers who, with a scintillating rhetoric, would be reading just about at halftime, if he wanted to come listen.

In what seemed to be his first hour of a long shift ahead, R. Williams looked at me for a few moments with some concern, as if he should have understood what I told him or simply brushed it off as another gate-crasher's futile scheme. I felt certain, if I could only jog his slow memory, that his lieutenant must have briefed him over their morning coffee and donuts about the Vistas of the Word reading and its esteemed participant authors. Despite the half-eaten ham sandwich in my lap, I certainly looked official, but appearances can only get you so far on game day, let alone on the biggest game day in years. Even if I didn't have a legitimate reason to proceed beyond the concrete barriers, I knew down inside, if I had wanted, I could have talked my way in. Back in college, gate-crashing had been a hobby of mine. All it took were easy white lies, the kind good salesmen told nightly in the bars of Holiday Inns and Marriotts across America. Typically, I would pose as a reviewer on assignment to cover a show. If asked about my rag, all I had to do was choose a modifier for the word *Review* that matched what I would assume to be the bouncer's level of intelligence, perhaps something like *Thunderbird Review* or, if necessary, something arty-sounding like *The Rothko Review of Arts & Letters*. I typically said such things quickly, with poor articulation resembling a speech affectation, to be sure nothing was completely understood but mutually acknowledged. And I'd always be sure to finish by reminding the bouncer that I understood perfectly what he had to go through sometimes when the people "upstairs" (even if it were only a one-story place) made his job difficult (the clincher).

R. Williams told me again, "Parking here is reserved for the game," by which I knew he meant reserved for those Big Donors who had better things to eat than ham sandwiches.

"But I'm the poet! A featured reader!" I complained. "I was told by the people upstairs that there would be a reserved spot for me when I arrived." I became a bit worried when R. Williams got on his walkie-talkie to mumble something that sounded like "fucking asshole," though after a few more moments he waved me through, pointing me toward a back lot on the opposite side of the stadium. Once past the concrete barriers and a field of Porta-Potties, I felt my status rise above the hot-dog eaters and T-shirt hawkers on the other side. In a lot to my left, there were rows and rows of media vans—CNN, CBS, NBC, ABC, FOX, ESPN—their antennae raised high like periscopes in enemy waters. Surely, I thought, they might be interested in the commentary of a poet. To my right, the Big Donors barbecued like fans on Lindsey, only here they had electric generators to run television sets around which they huddled in lawn chairs with their feet propped up on their beer coolers.

As R. Williams had directed, I kept on toward the back lot. I polished off the rest of my ham somewhere past the high-rise dorms while I searched for that elusive parking space reserved,

I had thought, in my name. Eventually I had to park in an unmarked spot. I felt cheated. As one of the featured writers, an esteemed wordsmith, at least in my own mind, I deserved a reserved space, especially considering all I had gone through in my limited career to get there—all the bad poems, all the misunderstood but truly profound lines, all the unappreciated allusions, all those years of rejections and form letters that began with "I regret to inform you" and ended with a heartfelt "Sincerely." Irate and thirsty from the Rolaids and ham, I could have almost canceled my big reading, though my first sight of Peter Donahue inside the conference center assuaged my temper considerably.

"It's crazy out there," I explained.

"Just like old times," he said.

It was the first time I had seen Peter in a number of years. Other than the few new lines of wisdom across his forehead, he looked much the same, a tall, somewhat husky fellow who, with thinning blond hair, looked something similar to Larry Bird. In fact, Peter has a passion for basketball like some do football. He even keeps himself in shape playing pickup games at lunch with what I assume must be other tall faculty and students at Birmingham-Southern College. For a number of years, Peter lived in Norman while his wife, now an attorney, taught on the faculty at OU. During this time, he planted trees in their yard a few blocks off Lindsey, worked on the book that would become *The Cornelius Arms*, and completed a Ph.D. up the highway at Oklahoma State. We met our first year in Stillwater, where we were students. Already well versed in the literary profession from his wife, Peter led the way and I followed. At times he was so brilliant that I thought he should be teaching the classes. It felt good to see him again, especially on a day in Norman marked with so much excitement and anticipation, perhaps a significant day in American collegiate football history.

At some point, after catching up a bit, I told Peter about my room at the Hampton Inn and how lucky I was to get it. He concurred, wishing he himself were staying somewhere other than at the Sooner Inn, with its lumpy beds and distance from the restaurants. However, neither of our stories compared with that of a managing editor from a reputable university press, who told us of having to take the only available room at a Ramada Inn, which was, of all things, attached to a barbecue restaurant. "Everything I brought with me is now smoked," she explained with scorn. "Can you smell it?" she asked, holding out her sleeve. I wanted to tell her about that small airplane pulling the "Do the Q" banner I'd seen early that morning but decided against it. As if the invitation to whiff an editor's clothing weren't bad enough, she then told us about the Ramada's hotel bar with its women's mud wrestling and fifty-dollar specials to rub oil on the wrestlers. Without pause, she transitioned smoothly to a description of her latest anthology of essays by feminist nature writers. "It would be great for your classes," she said, but all I could think about was smoked brisket and the big game.

Most of the morning up to the kickoff passed quietly, without so much as a sigh from anybody attending the readings. Inside the center, where they maintained the temperature at a sticky seventy-eight degrees Fahrenheit, we might have been anywhere but in Norman, Oklahoma, on the biggest day since Barry Switzer resigned in June of '89 amid players' scandals involving charges of gang rape, guns, and drugs, and an NCAA three-year probation for recruiting violations (some years later, in August of '97, authorities at the DFW Airport arrested Switzer himself for having a loaded revolver in his carry-on baggage). In fact, I might never have had the chance to experience any of the day's hysteria had Peter not suggested we get something to eat before our reading. "Do you have any idea what's going on out there?" I asked.

"As long as it's not halftime, the streets will be deserted. There's a Subway Sandwich just across from the Stadium. We'll be fine," he told me.

Like Dante, I followed where he led, past tailgaters glued

to their television screens, past the clatter of gas-powered generators, past the media lot, past countless grills with innumerable hot dogs, past empty beer cans and discarded cups, past the lines at the Porta-Potties. Every so often we heard cheers escaping from the stadium. At the corner of Jenkins and Lindsey, catty-corner from the men's athletic dorms and across from the end zone, we found ourselves in a crowd of students so thick it became difficult to make our way to the sandwich shop. College coeds in various states of euphoria and undress pressed in from all sides as policemen mounted on horses tried to keep the peace. I tried hard to remember my marriage vows, keeping my eyes off pierced bellies and skimpy low-cut bikini tops. At the entrance to the dorms, a ten-foot-high stage with a twenty-foot big-screen and an even larger inflated balloon resembling a giant bag of Tostitos tortilla chips towered over the students. Music from 107.7 KRXO's amplifiers drowned out any chance for a play-by-play. I had to remind myself that I was at a football game and not a Kiss concert, that I wasn't eighteen with an uncontrollable libido, that I was now middle-aged and respectfully repressed.

The line at Subway was out the door, not for the sandwiches but the ladies' room. Despite the parking lot full of Porta-Potties, Subway appeared to be the restroom of choice for nubile coeds with inconspicuous tattoos on their ankles, shoulder blades, and other discreet areas of their elastic bodies. Although these were not women of a Maori tribe, they belonged to a tribe of another sort: American youth. In my day, which wasn't all that long ago, tattoos were rare for women who weren't barmaids; they were largely for truckers and sailors (or "squids" as we affectionately called them). However, somebody, perhaps Dennis Rodman's agent, figured out how to turn tattoos into a ubiquitous fashion trait, along with nose rings, nipple rings, and rings for places too painful to type about. In the spirit of those first Western sailors to reach New Zealand and spy the island's women, I must admit to realizing then something licentious and erotic about the tattoo, perhaps the very mark of the forbidden. I tried hard to keep my mind on my order and my eyes from jumping, as the line in back of me swelled with a dozen uniformed Boy Scouts and their leader from the Last Frontier Council, who turned to me with a look that beckoned for a conversation with an adult civilian, albeit an incognito, libidinous poet.

"J. C. Watts," he volunteered, "is at the game with Barry Switzer."

"Congressman Watts?" I said.

"And former OU QB," Peter added. Watts, a resident of Norman who spends most of his time in DC, had commanded Switzer's wishbone offense to two Orange Bowls in '80 and '81 before going on to win the Canadian Football League's Grey Cup MVP for Ottawa in his '81 rookie year. As an African-American Bible-Belt conservative, he is an anomaly akin to Clarence Thomas, whom few Oklahomans will forget because of Anita Hill's sexual harassment allegations against him, which included his infamous crack about pubic hair in his Coke. Hill herself once taught law not far from the men's athletic dorms, where, at the end of the Switzer era, there were charges of gang rape, a shooting between players, and a quarterback's arrest for possession of cocaine.

"Maybe we should tell the congressman to do us a favor and step down from office," I returned, then realized I was in hostile territory, surrounded by conservative troop leaders, bladder-heavy coeds and hungry Scouts, all ready, if necessary, to take me down. "Just kidding," I said. "What brings you all to the game? Are you picking up trash?"

"Just helping old ladies cross the street," he said with a deadpan delivery I greatly admired.

"That's nice," I told him, as I ordered a turkey sub with lots of mayo and mustard.

"Actually," he continued, "we help with crowd control and parking. We've been coming here on game days for years.

Myself since 1976. It's part of the boys' community service. Yourself?"

"I'm a poet," I told him, paying the cashier. "I'm part of the halftime entertainment."

"Then good luck," he said. "You'll need it."

"Go Sooners!" I told him, grabbing my sandwich and large drink cup from the cashier.

I made my way over to the beverage dispenser then filled my giant cup with enough Diet Pepsi to ensure a trip to the Porta-Potties on my way back to the conference center. Surprisingly, I found a vacant table adjacent to the line for the ladies' room. Peter soon followed. As we ate, I thought about my wife and baby girl scooping up the bargains at what must have been a vacant Fashion Square Mall. As long as the big game was close, the streets and mall would remain deserted. Outside Subway, an Elvis impersonator (the Vegas years) wandered about the crowd along with frat boys, one with a big red O painted on his bare chest and his buddy with a large U. From our seats, I could see the CNN news team setting up their camera for a shot of the wild crowd who watched the mammoth big-screen in front of the giant Tostitos bag. Above it all, a helicopter circled, and not long after came that small plane again: "Bob's BBQ, Do the Q." As we watched the spectacle around us, the line for the john seemed to grow longer and longer, until it twisted out the door and into the closed-off street littered with empty beer cans.

"What do you plan to read?" I asked Peter, talking loud enough to be heard over the KRXO loudspeakers.

"A story about insanity," he told me. "You know it, 'The President Walks Home,' the one about the pressman who loses it after being fired."

"That's a great one," I told him, "especially his speech, 'Pull together.'"

"You?"

"A number of pieces from my book, 'The Bullet Hole in the

Wall at Bruff's Tavern,' 'Gina'—the one about the stripper—maybe even my newfound poem on women's underwear, 'The Eighth Wonder of the World.' For years," I explained, "I would go shopping with my wife and at some point I would find myself in the lingerie department with nothing to do but stand on its fringe and avert my eyes. Then it hit me; the poetry in the language of lingerie. How had I missed it all those years? I've always been an admirer of lingerie, silks and rayons, see-thrus and push-ups, cups and hooks, clasps and straps named after foods like spaghetti—something Italian, edible, filled with a latent sense of passion. While my wife was in the dressing room, I surreptitiously broke the label off some panties and began scratching product names on the backside. When it comes to lingerie, so much depends upon a red bra, on color, the tactile senses, on imagination. Can I talk about these things here?"

"Boy Scouts," Peter reminded me, "remember the Boy Scouts."

"Maybe we should talk football," I returned. Remembering my need to boost my immunity frequently when traveling, I took the sizeable 1000-mg vitamin C caplet from my pocket, then washed it down with some Diet Pepsi.

"What's there to talk about, the Switzer years, allegations of rape and guns in the men's dorms? Do you have a headache?"

"Vitamin C," I explained. "Never leave home without it."

"Are you a writer or a nut?"

When we had finished our sandwiches, it was time to return to our own big event, Vistas of the Word, before halftime made it impossible to move in any direction. As we walked out Subway's glass door, the CNN cameras positioned on the street corner began to light, then tape their reporter, a young woman with shoulder-length black hair, who stood surrounded by a frantic mass of screaming coeds and frat boys in torn crimson shirts. As she narrated a scene needing no comment, the mob about her furiously shook their erected index fingers at the camera, boys carried girls on their backs, and all of them jumped about slapping high fives with one another. The young reporter tried her best to keep her composure and feet steady in the shifting crowd.

Before heading for the conference center, we wandered over to the edge of the swelling, perhaps our biggest mistake of the day. On the Tostitos stage, where at halftime there would be a comedian to entertain this ticketless mass, the giant inflated bag of Tostitos rolled about in the wind, its guy lines straining to keep it down. The announcer's voice echoed about the stadium. The crowd around us quickly grew larger and larger until we found ourselves no longer on its fringe but closer to its pulsing center, caught in its undulating waves as if in a strong riptide with no way out. Looking up, I saw yet again that small plane crisscrossing the sky just beyond the stadium: "Bob's BBQ, Do the Q." In the mix, I became separated from Peter, who, swept up in the circle, floated away. After a large cheer from inside the stadium, everybody, including me, turned toward the twenty-foot big-screen, where, speechless, we watched the giant-sized Sooners, under Josh Heupel's command, drive the ball toward the Huskers' end zone. Soon I found myself with no way out, immersed in a rolling mass pressed tightly together, smothered in the crowd's core. I let my body move with those around me, young coeds bumping and rubbing against me without the slightest modesty. Amid this bubbling crowd, I began to understand the importance of autumn's Friday nights, those Saturday and Sunday afternoons. I felt something magical happening, too, a *joie de vivre* surfacing in me that I hadn't felt in years, something catching like the taste for barbecue, something racing in my veins, as if at any moment I could have thrown my blazer high over my head, ripped off my shirt and painted my chest with a big bloody O. The reading, if indeed I would make it there, seemed the farthest thing from my mind—what was poetry anyway but shadows on the wall of a cave?

When the Sooners ran the ball on the next play, their hard bodies galloping into one another for a touchdown, the tense young crowd encircling us erupted—"SOO-NERS! SOO-NERS!" they shouted, the band drumming, the brass blowing wildly. Whisked off my feet by an unbridled force, I too began to jump up and down with the near-naked, pierced-bellied girls and bare-chested boys screaming around me. "GO SOONERS!" I howled at the top of my lungs, a cry freer and more satisfying than any I had yelled in years—"GO, GO, GO!"

REMEMBER, SHE SAID, THE MAGIC

Disneyland is dedicated to the ideals, the dreams, and the hard facts that have created America ... with the hope that it will be a source of joy and inspiration to all the world.

—Walter Elias Disney, July 17, 1955

There are some places to which you vow never to return, then there are others about which you have no choice. "Everybody loves Disneyland," my Anaheim in-laws had told me, unaware of the troubling Disney memories that had haunted me for some thirty years. On our short ride to the park's front gates from the relatively new and mammoth Mickey & Friends parking structure on the Mickey & Friends tram, where we were warned about the dangers of standing and of body parts protruding beyond the vehicle, I wanted badly to connect with the family-in-law's enthusiasm and the other passengers' bonhomie. The closer we approached the park, the more I felt an uncomfortable anxiety, a discomforting sense of déjà vu that compelled me to turn back. Had my baby daughter not been present, I might have jumped, perhaps flung myself into the way of an oncoming tram, giving park-goers something they would never forget—I've always been attracted to the hideous and dramatic. Once through the front gates, we'd all read the motto above the archway of the park's surrounding berm: "Here you leave today and enter the world of yesterday, tomorrow, and fantasy," but instead I felt the true pain in nostalgia and knew all too well the undercurrents of danger lurking about the Snow White topiary and the Rivers of America.

Perhaps an omen: on our way into the Mickey & Friends parking structure, we had already survived a near collision with a Jerry Brown–era Volvo that cut across traffic, almost side-swiping our Pontiac Grand Am rental. I had my chance to turn around then, to spoil the family outing to save myself, but I continued onward to confront my demons. Before our trip began, I had consulted the Disneyland Website, which only furthered my anxiety with the following advice: "Come prepared for the unexpected." Despite my apprehensions, I did what I could to ensure magic at the Magic Kingdom: I filled three sixteen-ounce water bottles; packed a camera with two extra rolls of film; stuffed Pampers, sanitary wipes, saltines, and sunblock into our diaper bag; loaded my pocket with a handful of ibuprofen; popped a megadose of vitamin C; gathered extra clothes and cash for my wallet; and made us all ham sandwiches for lunch (against Disney prohibitions regarding the carrying of food into the park). The one item I forgot to put into our trunk, a stroller for our baby, would cost me in rental a good amount of what I'd saved in sandwiches and nearly half the actual cost of our idle lightweight model left behind in my mother-in-law's living room. I was sure Charlotte, the twelve-year veteran worker who scanned my credit card for the rental, had a hearty laugh every time she swiped a Visa for seven dollars a pop. "Remember," she said, "the Magic," her only words like something from an oracle. Then she pointed to her Kodak film button, handed me back my credit card, receipt, and an official Disney stroller checklist with ten boldly printed rules.

Stowing beneath the stroller's seat what bags we couldn't fit into a locker that I also regrettably had to rent, I tried hard to do as Charlotte suggested. I felt, however, a guilty pleasure in knowing we had received, from generous friends who worked at the park, free entry during what was a record-breaking spring break crowd, our savings roughly $205 ($43 per adult; $33 per child over three; free to children under three). Considering the cost, and for some families the years of saving for their trip, we might have been guilty of a gross violation of some unspoken Mouse ethos, as if we deserved exclusion from the park the same way men with long hair and those with unseemly tattoos, alternative lifestyles, or inappropriate clothing were once forbidden or discouraged from entering Walt's dreamland. But our savings alone were not enough to assuage my anxiety when I saw Sleeping Beauty's Castle looming in the distance just past the Lost Children Center. Lost Children was no park attraction, but Disneyland's very real limbo for the unfortunately separated, a place branded into my memory for its significance to my personal and familial saga, an unforgettable place for all the wrong reasons.

By the time we made our initial way up Main Street USA (ours back home in Kansas was destroyed by the Wal-Mart off I-35, Exit 128), we already had the first good hour under our belt. If I had calculated our trip's hourly rate up to that point, a trip that would unfortunately end two hours hence, we theoretically gave up in entry fees (albeit free), actual parking costs, and our locker and stroller rental approximately $72 per hour. For the family-in-law, who stood holding hands together in front of Central Plaza's bronze statue of Walt and his little mouse pal, money seemed the furthest thing from their minds. They were experiencing a moment of joy, a triumphant return to where they had visited as a happy family many times over the years, a magic kingdom where the day was truly theirs, where, as Walt declared in his opening-day dedication, a place where "age relives fond memories of the past." I, however, associated the park with a nausea I suffer from anything that spins in circles, my distaste for crowds, and especially my family experience thirty years ago when we lost my then-five-year-old younger brother in the shuffle exiting The Walt Disney Story attraction.

I believe this deleterious event and my brother's accompanying experience in the limbo of Lost Children severely compromised our lives forever after. For my brother, the trauma had what I consider to be a long-term psychological impact, perhaps manifesting itself in him in ways similar to what we know of the lives of Roger Clinton or Billy Carter. I, on the other hand, had been able to repress the memory, the impact less on the surface of my psyche and more in the depths of my twisted subconscious where originate fetishes and appetites too risqué to disclose in this family essay. I write of this dark day not to further aggravate my brother's problems, cause him nightmares, or trigger for him any post-traumatic stress incidents, but because of the park's importance to my in-laws, who cherish their Disneyland visits as celebrations of family unity. In other words, if ever I hoped to be fully accepted into this Disney-loving family, if Disneyland were to continue to draw us together over the years, and if I were ever to feel the way millions of other Americans do for this park in their personal and cultural memories, I had to overcome the past.

As the family-in-law beamed, I tried hard to turn my frown upside down. Maybe it wasn't possible to change my attitude or reprogram my memory. Then again, maybe I had to give myself up to the swollen spring break crowd that smelled as a whole like coconut tanning oil, submit to Disney with a Jerry Lewis–like commitment to the magic, and muster a sense of enthusiasm similar to Ronald Reagan's on Disneyland's opening day, July 17, 1955, as he cohosted the ABC live *Dateline: Disneyland* TV broadcast with Bob Cummings (*Love That Bob*) and Art Linkletter (*House Party*). Perhaps like them I could find common ground in my past, in what I actually liked about Disney, besides how women on Main Street USA, lost their high heels in the fresh asphalt on opening day, a.k.a. "Black Sunday." As kids, my brother and I had been taken with Disney movies such as *Mary Poppins* (still a personal favorite), *The Absent-Minded Professor* (we wanted Fred MacMurray to be our dad), and Kurt

Russell films with tin-sounding voice tracks such as *The Barefoot Executive* and *The Strongest Man in the World*. We had even dreamed of moving to Medfield. I also remember how together we watched Sunday's *Wonderful World of Disney* eating TV dinners on TV trays—Salisbury steak with mashed potatoes, mixed vegetables, and a square dessert assumed to be apple pie.

A product of the Brady Bunch generation, I knew I was supposed to love Disney, Ronald Reagan, Michael Eisner, and the Mouse. I had to believe, for the sake of my baby girl, my wife's Disney-loving family, and perhaps even for my own dear brother, that I was still capable of such Disney-inspired love, a spirit powerful enough to melt the most hardened or dysfunctional heart. In theory, I love many things. I love California (when not crowded). I love orange juice (if not from concentrate). I love burritos (even the frozen kind). I love wine (despite my income). I love the Beach Boys (with no reservations). I love my wife (who doesn't love the Beach Boys). I love my daughter (who already loves "Barbara Ann"). I love some people (as long as they don't stand too close or cough on me). I love tattoos (on others). I love my neighbor with the leased Chevy pickup (well, mostly just the stag head on his apartment wall). I love abstract art (especially when with those who say, "I don't get it"). I love movies (except gratuitous action and horror flicks). I love musicals (and the color pink). I love the idea of amusement parks (just not *actual* amusement parks). And I love feeling happy (as long as it doesn't cost me money).

As we stood in front of Central Plaza's bronzed statue of Walt and his little mouse pal—my twenty-one-month-old baby girl mesmerized by the sheer size of the sculpture—I placed my hand over my heart (and would have kneeled if it had been appropriate) to make that necessary commitment all park-goers must, especially if they want to leave the park feeling as if their money bought them something pleasantly unforgettable, that wonderful kind of unforgettable, perhaps with a cinnamon scent, of which memories should be made. If possible, I would have had Reverend Glenn Puder lead me in prayer, the way he did Walt and his friends on Disneyland's opening day, and Walt's brother, Herbert, into wedded bliss. Before Walt and Mickey, I vowed to enjoy myself, despite my long litany of reservations and despite the haunting memory of that frantic search for my brother in the unruly crowd exiting The Walt Disney Story those many years ago. The entire family-in-law seemed already well under the Disney spell, ready for cotton candy, snow cones, popcorn, frozen yogurt, their own Mouse ears, and to stand in lines no matter what the length. Saluting Walt and Little Mickey, I too felt ready to give the park another try.

Given that we were traveling with my wheelchair-bound mother-in-law, two small children, and an adult (that's me) who becomes nauseated on most rides, we decided to stick to attractions such as "it's a small world" (sic) that relied more on sentiment and overwhelming detail than on the cheap thrills of spins, dips, and whiplash turns. Making our way toward Fantasyland, past Sleeping Beauty's Castle, past the Mad Tea Party, past the Storybook Land Canal Boats, toward "it's a small world," I felt a strange euphoria bubbling in my blood. Most of my appreciation and sense of well-being swelled from my brother-in-law's deep knowledge of the park, the way Mr. Roarke knew Fantasy Island or Captain Stubing his Love Boat. As crowds and characters (officially, Disney castmembers) swelled about us, I understood that, to truly appreciate the park on physical, cerebral, and spiritual levels, one had to look past the large attractions to Disneyland's seemingly infinite maze constructed of the very finest details. Somehow, I felt that if I were able to master its design, I would gain a greater sense of security, a feeling of being in control that might help alleviate my childhood memories of helplessness and guilt over losing my younger brother.

Some of what you must know for a fuller park experience, or a false sense of being in control: Hidden Mickeys (silhouettes of Sir Mouse etched and painted onto obvious and obscure places in the park that are celebrated and accounted for in fan clubs around the world); old A-E ticket booths used before general admission tickets became the industry standard (some have been razed, while others have been turned into props on attraction sets); the Disneyland Railroad's "Lilly Belle" (Walt's very own caboose reserved for Disney executives, their privileged guests, or lucky tourists); a basketball court inside at the top of the Matterhorn Bobsleds mountain; hidden security cameras throughout the park (occasionally women flash a camera when dropping through Splash Mountain); props from Disney films used in attractions; how the buildings on Main Street USA, and other places in the park shrink in scale from bottom to top to create a fantasy appearance; special tributes on Main Street USA windows and in attraction rides (for people such as the park's original Imagineers (designers) or Disney corporate leaders like Frank Wells); the prohibition against chewing gum sales; rules for castmember waving and costume changes (including recently amended regulations allowing the personal cleaning of costume underwear); and Club 33 (Walt's exclusive, private club rumored to be named after the park's first thirty-three investors, its trophy room's maximum capacity, or its location at 33 Royal Street in New Orleans Square. A single corporate membership at the time of this writing was $10,000 with substantial annual dues, but members receive free parking and admission to the park, except for special events or private parties. Members admitted to the park must, however, dine at Club 33 or be billed for the regular price of admission. Rumors run rampant about Club 33's decor, from hidden microphones to the wall art of Disney movie animation cells to a table used in the Mary Poppins movie. But more than one source notes how, when the Disney Corporation assumed control in the eighties, Mrs. Disney replaced all original works with copies. Club 33 is not listed in the "Disneyland Today" brochure map but can be found by those with a discerning eye; it also serves the only alcoholic drinks in the park); lastly, consider Disneyland's address, 1313

Harbor Boulevard (ask yourself as have others: Is M the thirteenth letter of the alphabet? Does MM stand for Mickey Mouse? What is MM backwards? Does 3 on its side look like mouse ears? Did Walt wish to keep away those with triskaidekaphobia? Is the address a Cold War code to the launching of our nuclear arsenal? Is the Matterhorn an incognito missile silo? Or was 1313 a slight to those who thought the park would fail?).

Disneyland's apparently infinite number of details seemed unaccountable or unverifiable even by the Disney Corporation itself, which often dismisses the more fantastic claims the way our government does alleged alien autopsies, Kennedy assassination conspiracy theories, the secret to Colonel Sanders Original Recipe, the whereabouts of Jim Morrison, or the real level of industrial pollutants dumped into our waterways or sprayed on our crops back in Kansas. The park tested the very boundaries of my ability to construct a determinable universe with any sense of cohesion and harmony. However, as our day progressed, I took an absurd pleasure in the uncomfortable unknowing, as if I were beginning to see a part of the big picture from its fragments. Perhaps this was all just a game with no larger puzzle to construct, something like the unverifiable rumors about Walt Disney's cryogenically frozen body. Nevertheless, understanding my brother's trauma meant trying to see the maze from a child's eyes, all the turns, corners, shadows, legs, tattooed ankles, big bellies, vendors, attractions, decorations, colors, neon, flashing lights, mirrors, gum on the sidewalk, discarded Popsicle wrappers, false fronts, and balloons floating away in the wind.

Walter Elias Disney seemed the true Wizard of Oz, the man behind the curtain pulling at the levers. From a groundswell of pessimism and naysayers, including Walt's brother who believed the Magic Kingdom stood no chance, Disneyland grew into a cultural icon, as much part of America as Sally Hemings. At the beginning on July 17, 1955, there were only five lands—Main Street USA, Adventureland, Frontierland, Tomorrowland, and Fantasyland—built on a roughly 160-acre orange grove, only the seeds of the mustard plant that grew and grew to encompass its latest additions and renovations; its landscaping, parking, and bathrooms; a pet kennel ($10 a day, but not overnight); an unofficial Gay Day each October (totally and thoroughly unsanctioned and in no way encouraged at all, anytime, anywhere, by Disney or any of its affiliates, etc., etc., etc., *but wear a red shirt*); a Gerber Baby Care Center complete with diaper machines, nursing areas, bottle warmers, and changing stations; and, of course, the shadowy Lost Children Center.

Everything had a story, a history, a significance, a price tag, a magic to be remembered—every attraction, every ride, an overwhelming sophistication. To truly know such magic necessitated giving oneself up to it while remembering the park's protean nature—as the weekly updated park map warns, "All information subject to change without notice."

The labyrinth, if entered, might lead nowhere—again, imagine it from a lost child's perspective or on a therapist's couch. If any ride seemed the epitome of this principle, it had to be "it's a small world," first known as the Pepsi-Cola Pavilion at the 1964 New York World's Fair. The only ride to tunnel through the berm, it is in and of itself (with its 578 individual details by one account, 550 estimated by Disney) its own metacommentary on the greater, more elaborate maze of which it is a part. When we found ourselves on the ride, I felt certain I had discovered a key. Assisting us with our seating on the gondola was Castmember Jenny, who wore a white shirt and royal blue slacks held snug against her trim waist with a special belt embroidered with the flags of the world. As we sailed off, the girls and I waved to Jenny from my seat at the bow, fully appreciating her mandatory smile and intricate uniform.

The seven-minute ride toured places resembling the Middle East, India, Asia, and Africa (represented by Pygmies) and culminated with a passage through the icy Arctic. Perhaps it was Epcot Center in miniature, or maybe there was something more sinister to the innocent worlds depicted. I tried to take a photo, but my wife quickly reminded me of the "no photographs" regulation. If I hadn't been with them, I would have taken the picture, despite rumors of a hidden castmember observing us from the Sentinel Tower. Around the world we went, though many times I questioned the course of navigation. While the chipper music rang out and the air conditioning blew over us, I felt there was something more to the ride that didn't make itself obvious; perhaps in the attraction's symbolism, in its arctic conclusion, there was an implicit world hierarchy.

Thirty years ago, I had left the ride with my brother, humming together its catchy tune (due to complications too numerous to cite, I had to delete the lyrics here—but you know how they go). Upon our return home, despite my brother's trauma, I even bought the piano sheet music that I played until my fingers ached. How long after the ride and the multiple playings of the song on wintry afternoons in our basement had I carried these intimations of the Disney World Order? How long did the music continue to be the soundtrack to my brother's recurring park nightmares?

As our gondola pulled into port, I tried to brush off my epiphany as a side effect of my literary profession. As Castmember Jenny wheeled my mother-in-law off the boat, I knew I had to try harder to fulfill my commitment to the bronzed Mouse and his Creator. The day was still pleasant, our little girls full of giggles, my wife and her mother without complaint, my brother-in-law still enthused enough to point out the remains of an old ticket booth in a bed of flowers.

Making our way to Toontown, I could feel the magic working. In what I had come to know about the park, I was more and more able to see it through my brother's eyes. My previous amusement-park malaise gave way slowly to a sense of greater euphoria, as if Disneyland pumped the park with extra oxygen to make everybody feel just a little bit better. "Caution: Gags Ahead," a sign warned. We took a few moments to look at our distorted reflections in the funny mirrors, then my little girl pressed her way through a crowd of kids to hug Goofy. I tried hard to keep my eye on her as she pushed through all the legs. I also tried not to think of the germs, the layers of snot about Goofy's waist, or the possibility of getting lice from his costume. There was an innocent pleasure in my baby's smile from the sheer sense of joy she felt in telling Goofy how much she loved him, the same sort of innocent satisfaction my brother must have known just before entering The Walt Disney Story. Maybe my toddler would consciously remember the encounter; if not, it would rest somewhere in her forming subconscious, providing her with a lifetime of Disney warmth, the entire park like a deep map, a small world, the right world, the Disney land. Watching her, I felt something similar surface in my blood— flashbacks of orange groves, a blue ocean and warm sand, the smell of cotton candy, the "It's a Small World" theme song, a vivid memory of my little brother and me riding together through Pirates of the Caribbean, his gentle smile only shortly before his life-changing trauma, his contentment riding securely with me, his feeling that I would be there for him for the rest of his life. That memory made me feel so good that I wanted for some odd reason to spend all of my money, every last unnecessary cent, as if by giving it all away I would be able to cast off the veneer of the adult world—a penny for every fountain, a tip to every castmember, a dollar for every kid, every parent, every seller of frozen chocolate bananas, ice-cream sandwiches, and mouse ears.

Outside Goofy's Bounce House, I took a seat on the curbside to rest while the family-in-law played about Toontown. A trolley passed and I waved to the families on board, who waved back at me without the reservations common to suburbanites or those that live in gated communities. Next to the Bounce House was a lovely plastic-looking garden that caught my attention; however, the seemingly quaint fakes were really growing—artichoke, parsley, lettuce, rosemary, cabbage, strawberry, oregano, chive, tomato, and more. The small, profuse garden seemed like a miracle in this place of fantasies. A lovely smell of basil floated about that omnipresent odor of coconut tanning oil. Though taken with the garden, the actuality of this detail, the real as a simulacrum to itself, I still couldn't get the dark side of Disney out of my mind, its thousands of lost children each year, and, perhaps more frightening, what I had learned about the eight tourists who, over the years, had met untimely deaths on park attractions—two by falling off the Matterhorn (1964 and 1984), one struck by the Monorail (1966), two crushed by the People Mover (1967 and 1980), two more by drowning in the Rivers of America (1973 and 1983), and one victim (1998) struck by a metal cleat that sprang loose from the *Columbia* sailing-ship dock on the Rivers of America. These deaths seemed almost unbelievable, as unbelievable as the idea that a lost child might not be found. These were unfortunate and unlikely incidents, some caused by the victim's own negligence, but some also random, chance moments. In a magical place like Disneyland, it was possible to believe that someone could suffer a deathblow and still rise again, like in cartoons and myths. But maybe beneath these attractions and wondrous sets was really a tar pit of dinosaur bones. It seemed that the only thing to do when the reach of Hades lurked so close was to give up unabashedly to Dionysus. From somewhere, I felt an urge to strip off my clothes, to revel with those around me already half naked, those desiring the same true liberation. Perhaps there was a way to get out the word, to plan a moment when there would be a mass streaking at Disneyland, an unofficial Birthday Suit Day like the unofficial Gay Pride Day, say at noon, July 1, each year, to celebrate the park's own birthday.

The magic in me seemed to grow and grow. Not long after Toontown, when I found myself in line with the family at the

Country Bear Playhouse, squeezed between two men larger than my armoire, I just didn't care. Under normal circumstances, I might have felt cramped by the thick-necked men with their expensive cameras or the woman of similarly large proportions behind them who straddled a motorized scooter (in Disneyspeak an "electric convenience vehicle," the kind reserved for the disabled in our local Wal-Mart). Cloaked in a red Disneyland sweatshirt over which hung a thirty-, maybe forty-inch gold rope chain of some thickness, the scooterwoman sweated profusely. I thought briefly about asking her if she might want some help to remove her sweatshirt, but decided with guilty pleasure against it. Given my situation, the ache of my back from standing for what already must have been a good twenty minutes, I continued to feel upbeat, ready for the Country Bear sing-along. My restless baby girl, chased by her mother, whirled about the many legs in the gathering crowd. When the theater doors swung open, I raced forward to save seats in the front row. By all measures, when they lowered the lights and the music began, we would have a spectacular view of the Country Bears jug band, which reminded me fondly of a previous family trip to Arkansas.

Then an unstoppable descent began, first with a stop-and-start whimper, followed by some tears, then a few moans, followed by our baby's all-out crying. My wife and I tried our best to comfort her, to hold our little girl snugly against us, trading her off like a lateraled football late in the fourth quarter. Outside the Country Bear Playhouse, in the stroller parking area, I had, against the stern warning on the stroller checklist, left all of our gear, including the pacifier. As our baby continued to cry, we thought of leaving the show; however, given our first-row seats and the difficulty in moving my mother-in-law's wheelchair, we decided to stick it out, believing the sing-along would cheer her up. But her crying soon led to other random outbursts, baby to baby, the way dog barking begins with a sole yelp then, dog by dog, consumes a quiet neighborhood; the noise spread until it seemed all the children were bawling despite those cheery Country Bears. *Remember,* I repeated to myself, *the Magic.* As my wife's frustration grew with all the other parents around us, I still felt pretty good, enough to stomp and slap along in time with the Country Bears. It was indeed a glorious moment, perhaps my finest of the day. With each song, each beat of that catchy country music, the better I felt, my dark memories turning lighter, until the show ended some ten minutes later and we spilled out of the Country Bear Playhouse with our child now weeping uncontrollably.

As everyone in the family-in-law took turns trying to calm her, I went forth to retrieve our stroller and pacifier, humming the "it's a small world" theme song. Without haste, I pulled the well-stowed gear from the stroller and began fumbling through the various bags; however, the pacifier was nowhere to be found. I tried again, this time spreading the gear piece by piece next to the stroller and only inches from that record-breaking crowd. *Remember the Magic. Remember the Magic.* Unable to locate the pacifier, I re-stuffed the stroller as best I could, our gear now hanging out precipitously, as if at any moment, piece by piece, everything would fall off and be gone forever. I looked at the previously well-stuffed stroller, stuffed so well, I had thought, as to discourage theft itself lest the pile mercilessly uncoil at the touch of the first red hand, then pushed the mess up a street thick with people. The family-in-law pleaded for the pacifier. "It's gone," I explained, our hysteric baby receiving passing stares from the unflustered on a Disney high who didn't appear as if they were coming down anytime soon.

"I thought you packed everything," my wife returned, "everything" meaning the pacifier or anything else we might have needed at that moment.

"Maybe it's in the locker back near The Walt Disney Story?"

The family-in-law stared in disbelief. Then my wife gave me one of those looks that wives only give just before coming completely undone.

Once again, it seemed The Walt Disney Story would undo me, again play a significant and unfortunate role in my family history. Some thirty years ago, outside The Walt Disney Story with my father and older brother, I wept at the thought of never finding my younger brother, my best of friends, my roommate who breathed contentedly each night in the bunk next to mine—those slings and arrows of outrageous fortune! Back then, before our California trip, we had been a happy family— happy families are all alike (especially at Disneyland). We still took family vacations, stopped at family roadside attractions like Stuckey's for pecan pie and souvenir cedar products, and listened as a family to my father proclaim stuff like "Families stick together" and "Nobody's closer than blood." I was almost seven. Until that moment in my life, long before my parents finally divorced twenty-five years later, the worst thing that had ever happened to me, besides the brace for my crooked foot or my inability to sleep when my parents did battle in the kitchen, was the death of some frogs I had captured at Blackey's pond in Wisconsin, where our family summered at cabins owned by Blackey, one of my father's clients.

Blackey's pond was my Rosebud, a childhood idyll where leafy birch overlooked a cedar-tinted pond that streamed into a large blue lake. While my brother says he has little memory of the long drive—*Are we there yet? Are we there yet?*—and those days at the lakeside cabin, I can recall spending summer after-noons with him looking for turtles and frogs, capturing grasshoppers and fishing for bluegills, boating with my father and watching stars glitter like fireflies across the lake's surface on a warm night. So indelible are these fond memories of fam-ily bliss I've imagined that, in my final bedridden moments, my last paroxysm will be *Blackey's!*

My baby girl still crying profusely and now refusing to sit in her stroller, my wife hurried her off toward the locker room at the front of the park in the hope of locating the pacifier. In the brief two years of her life, I had never seen our baby in such unstoppable hysterics, especially not in public, nor my tired wife so completely frustrated (then again, four days on the road without naps had taken its toll). My brother-in-law, who pushed my wheelchair-bound mother-in-law on whose lap sat her other granddaughter, pursued them. They seemed stunned at this relentless outburst, this tantrum of tantrums, and looked distraught but politely silent, something that would never, under any circumstance, have happened in my own immediate and vocal family.

The following is a list of attractions we passed (and would never experience) as my wife screamed at me, "Hurry your ass up!": Davy Crockett's Explorer Canoes, Splash Mountain, Disneyland Railroad, Haunted Mansion, Fantasmic! Viewing Area for Guests Using Wheelchairs, Rafts to Tom Sawyer Island, Kodak Photo Spot, the Disney Gallery, Club 33, Pirates of the Caribbean, Tarzan™'s Treehouse, Indiana Jones™ Adventure, Jungle Cruise, Character Location, Kodak Photo Spot (#2), Pay Telephones, Automated Teller Machine, Enchanted Tiki Room, Information Center, Fire Engine, Horse Drawn Street Cars, Bronzed Statue of Walt and Little Mickey (where I stopped briefly to genuflect), Rest Rooms, Kodak Photo Spot (#3), Baby Services (represented by pacifier icon), Lost Children Center (strong déjà vu), Parade Viewing Area for Guests Using Wheelchair, Lost and Found, Lockers (since our pacifier was not in the locker with the rest of the gear and since my baby girl's tantrum continued unabated, we continued onward) ... Main Street Cinema, Omnibus, The Walt Disney Story, featuring "Great Moments with Mr. Lincoln"—

Outside the theater, despite the pressure otherwise from the family-in-law, I paused. *Remember the Magic ... Remember the Magic ... Remember ... Remember ...* looking for my brother ... all the people ... all the legs ... all the pushing ... How could I have lost him? Why didn't he hold onto my hand? Where was my father? We searched everywhere, all the exits, inside and outside of the theater, calling out his name. It was as if he, or we, were trapped in a maze with no way out. How could we ever explain the loss of my brother to my mother, who had been happily shopping for bargains along Main Street USA? Unable to do anything other than follow my father as he circumnavigated the immediate area looking at every passing child in every smiling family, I felt flawed. For the first time in my life, I felt a conscious realization of my helplessness, that even my father was not always in control, that perhaps control itself were a fiction. Thinking back, I have difficulty remembering exactly how long we looked, but clearly it was a long, long time. In the moment of giving up our search, in the fear I recognized in my father's face, I felt something go out of each of us, something that perhaps never returned to our family on that day or on any other.

When we entered Lost Children, a scene now significantly distorted by memory but reconstituted here nonetheless, it must have seemed of Pinocchio-esque proportions—sobbing children, catatonic children, and hysteric children mixed with crying, stoic, and even angry parents. I gave each face a good look, but soon every face came to resemble my brother's—innumerable faces—so incredibly confusing. How could I not have seen him? Where could he have been? Then my father found him on Mickey's lap, his eyes crusted from his life-changing trauma. I felt so relieved in finding him that, not wanting to cry myself, I somehow broke into an uncontrollable fit of laughter. "Be thankful you found him," my father scolded.

As I stood for a second time in front of The Walt Disney Story, watching my flustered wife, our screaming baby, and the family-in-law exit the park without hand stamps, I couldn't help but give up another cathartic laugh, a bellyache, a giddiness that often comes upon me in moments of absurdity beyond my control. A few moments later, I too turned away from the park, but not without a new sense of well-being that I attributed to my purging of the uncomfortable past. If I had had a cell phone, I would have called my brother to let him know that I had seen the labyrinth from his eyes, that I should have held more tightly to his hand those many years ago, despite how my father blamed him for not sticking with us.

Beyond the berm at the front gates, the contents of our rented locker spilling from my arms, I stopped to get my hand stamped, though I knew we would not be returning that day. Across the plaza, I could see the rust-colored Golden Gateway bridge of Disney's California Adventure, an entire new park for another day. The family-in-law, all of whom were now well past the breaking point, waited impatiently for me to catch up. I walked toward them with a sense of inner calm I hadn't felt in years. While they brimmed with frustration, I desired to embrace them all at once. After just three hours in the park, we boarded the tram to return us to the magnificent Mickey & Friends parking structure.

At the elevator and escalators to the Goofy section where we parked, I watched my wife, who was not speaking to me, take our still-crying baby and the family-in-law up to our cars. *Remember*, I wanted to say, *the Magic*, as if it were a mantra to inner tranquility. I would meet up with them after a brief stop to use the restroom. Standing at the urinal, I looked about the large, vacant room, where I thought I saw in the wall's mosaic tile a Hidden Mickey. If only my brother-in-law were with me, he might have been able to verify the sighting. Just for fun, I felt like mooning the spot where I thought the hidden security cameras were located, something my brother would have wanted me to do in his honor, but I stopped short of doing anything too crazy in a Disneyland restroom where children with their fathers could enter at any moment (I know firsthand how a childhood trauma at the park can stick with a person for life). I was a grown man now, I told myself, no longer a boy on a family vacation, leading my own family (or some fantasy like that).

After washing my hands, I gave my face a few good braces. I ran some water through my hair, then took a good look in the mirror, the lines growing deeper in my forehead, a touch of gray here and there. All things considered, I felt good, really pretty damn good, a guilty kind of good that only a family man alone in a public restroom can properly feel. I had entered and exited the great labyrinth, and it was time again to head home to the Kansas outback. After a few more sacred moments to myself, I stepped out of the bathroom into the bright light to ride the escalator up to the good life I'd come to make for myself in the world.

I drove the easily flowing carpool lane home to my in-laws' while the baby slept soundly in her car seat, sucking her treasured pacifier that in the coming months she would reluctantly give up, the way we must all learn to let things go. Passing through the smoggy sprawl of Anaheim, I wondered if there were still any citrus groves left like the ones I remembered picking oranges from with my brother. That night I would give him a long-overdue call, let him know about his niece's first trip to the park, and plan the next time we might get together. As I zipped along in the carpool lane eating a ham sandwich, my wife lapsed into a nap. Perhaps she dreamed of riding the Storybook Land Canal Boats with her father, or maybe she dreamed of feeling as rested as she once did before becoming a mother. Then the melody of "When You Wish Upon a Star" came to me, as if it were my very own theme song (we all need one). I heard it begin slowly then rise ever so gently with a mellifluous timbre, the velvety, reassuring vocals of Cliff Edwards's Jiminy Cricket, singing about the guiding hand of fate. In the brief peace of that late afternoon, in one of those evanescent moments when things seem for the briefest of time in their proper places, I hummed my theme music like a bluebird. I felt so good, I could have kept driving, perhaps all the way back to Kansas. Some year, on another visit to the in-laws, I knew our families would return to the Magic Kingdom—we just had to—

it was coded deep in our blood and now in the blood of one in whom our blood freely mingled.

Fade out with long shot of car on crowded freeway that begins to sail above the traffic up to a bright blue sky.

Roll credits to theme music.

NOTES

Works are cited in the general order that they are referenced in each chapter.

Out Here in the Out There

Willa Cather. *O Pioneers!* Boston: Houghton Mifflin, 1913, p. 38.

Theresa Jensen Lacey. *The Pawnee.* New York: Chelsea House, 1996, pp. 13–14.

Kenneth Lincoln. *Men Down West.* Santa Barbara, CA: Capra, 1997.

Peter Stitt. "Interview with William Stafford." In *The World's Hieroglyphic Beauty: Five American Poets.* Athens: University of Georgia Press, 1985, p. 96.

How I Learned to Shoot Straight

Hunter S. Thompson. "An Interview with Sarah Nelson." In *The Book Report* (www.thebookreport.com), 1997. Reprinted in *Far Gone Books* (www.fargonebooks.com).

William S. Burroughs. "The War Universe." *Grand Street* 37 (1992): 93–108.

Subsequent to the writing of this essay, Bruff's Bar and Grill burned down in a fantastic blaze. The fire station was only one block away.

Parable of the Spiny-Toothed Gumweed

William Allen White. "Kansas: A Puritan Survival." 1922. Reprinted in Thomas Fox Averill, ed., *What Kansas Means to Me: Twentieth-Century Writers on the Sunflower State.* Lawrence: University Press of Kansas, 1991, p. 62.

Charles Dickens. *Hard Times.* 1854. Introduction and edited by David Craig. New York: Penguin, 1985, p. 65.

Epiphania

Neil Young. "Albuquerque." *Tonight's the Night*. Warner Brothers, 1975.

The billboard referenced was erected by the Los Alamos Study Group (LASG), a group of antinuclear activists under the direction of Greg Mello (see www.lasg.org). For more information contact the LASG at 212 E. Mercy St., Suite 10, Santa Fe, NM 87501.

"The Kansas Fool" by C. S. Whitney (sung to gospel hymn "Beulah Land"). In *The Alliance and Labor Songster: A Collection of Labor and Comic Songs for the Use of Alliances, Debating Clubs, Political Gatherings*. Compiled by Leopold Vincent. Winfield, KS: H. & L. Vincent Printers, 1890.

Hart Crane. *The Bridge*. 1930. New York: Liveright, 1992.

T. S. Eliot. *The Waste Land*. 1922. In *The Waste Land and Other Poems*. New York: Signet, 1998.

Ezra Pound. "E.P. Ode pour L'Election de Son Sepulchre." In *Hugh Selwyn Mauberly: Life and Contacts*. London: Ovid Press, 1920.

Simon Ortiz. *From Sand Creek: Rising in This Heart Which Is Our America*. New York: Thunder's Mouth, 1981.

Robert Creeley. "I Know a Man." In *Collected Poems of Robert Creeley, 1945–1975*. Berkeley and Los Angeles: University of California Press, 1982.

Allen Ginsberg. "A Supermarket in California." In *Collected Poems 1947–1980*. New York: Harper, 1984.

Vladimir Nabokov. *Speak, Memory: An Autobiography Revisited*. 1967. Rev. ed. of *Conclusive Evidence*. 1951. New York: Vintage, 1989, pp. 217, 218.

John Ashbery. "The Instruction Manual." In *Selected Poems*. New York: Penguin, 1986.

"Now we're all sons of bitches" is widely attributed to Kenneth Bainbridge and "I am become Death, the shatterer of worlds" to J. Robert Oppenheimer after witnessing the first successful test of a nuclear bomb at the Trinity Test Site, July 16, 1945, The Oppenheimer quotation has been traced to the *Bhagavad-Gita*.

Medilogue: Introduction to an American Outback

William Least Heat-Moon. *PrairyErth (A Deep Map)*. Boston: Houghton Mifflin, 1991, pp. 11–12, 28, 77.

Larry McMurtry. *Roads: Driving America's Great Highways*. New York: Simon and Schuster, 2000, p. 44.

Henry David Thoreau. *Walden and Other Writings*. 1854. Edited by Joseph Wood Krutch. New York: Bantam, 1982, pp. 172, 329, 330, 319.

Yi-Fu Tuan. *Topophilia: A Study of Environmental Perception, Attitudes, and Values*. Englewood Cliffs, NJ: Prentice Hall, 1974, p. 93.

Edward Abbey. *Desert Solitaire: A Season in the Wilderness*. New York: Ballantine, 1968, pp. 6, 221.

Storm data post-1950 compiled from the archive of the National Climatic Data Center (NCDC), the self-described "World's Largest Archive of Weather Data" (see www.ncdc.noaa.gov/oa/ncdc.html). Information on tornadoes in Kansas prior to 1950 came in part from the comprehensive Tornadochaser.com database compiled by Tim Baker at www.tornadochaser.com/torhist3.htm. Such severe-weather data often varies between sources due to differences in reporting, accounting, and in defining storm paths as they move through various geographic locations.

Larry Schwarm. *On Fire*. Center for Documentary Study. Durham, NC: Duke University Press/Lyndhurst Books, 2003.

Stephen J. Pyne. *Fire in America*. Seattle: University of Washington Press, 1982.

Scott Richardson. "Metascrawl." *Flint Hills Review* 8 (2003): 54.

Scott Richardson. "In Kansas." *Tales Out of School*. Center for Great Plains Studies. March 2003: 1–2.

Carl L. Becker. "Kansas." In *Essays in American History Dedicated to Frederick Jackson Turner*. New York: Henry Holt, 1910. Reprinted in Thomas Fox Averill, ed., *What Kansas Means to Me: Twentieth Century Writers on the Sunflower State*. Lawrence: University Press of Kansas, 1991, p. 22.

Scott Richardson. "Midnight Mischief." *Flint Hills Review* 8 (2003): 55.

Curious Abrupt Questionings: The Lure of Glitz and Glam

Walt Whitman. "Crossing Brooklyn Ferry." In *Leaves of Grass* (9th edition, 1892). New York: New American Library, 1958.

Tom Wolfe, "Las Vegas (What?) Las Vegas (Can't hear you! Too noisy) Las Vegas!!!!" In *The Kandy-Kolored Tangerine-Flake Streamline Baby*. New York: Farrar, Straus and Giroux, 1965. Reprinted in Mike Tronnes, ed., *Literary Las Vegas: The Best Writing about America's Most Fabulous City*. New York: Holt, 1995, p. 5.

Michael Ventura. "Las Vegas: The Odds on Anything." In *Letters at 3 AM: Reports on Endarkenment*. Dallas: Spring Publications, 1993. Reprinted in Mike Tronnes, ed., *Literary Las Vegas: The Best Writing about America's Most Fabulous City*. New York: Holt, 1995.

The Green Burrito

Ray Gonzalez. "Praise the Tortilla, Praise Menudo, Praise Chorizo." In *The Heat of Arrivals*. Rochester, NY: Boa Editions, 1996.

Information in part obtained from Kenneth F. Kiple and Kriemhild Coneè Ornelas. *The Cambridge World History of Food*. Cambridge: Cambridge University Press, 2000. Material on chilies adapted from "Chili Peppers" by Jean Andrews, pp. 281–287. Material on tomatoes adapted from "Tomatoes" by Janet Long, pp. 351–358. Material on maize adapted from "Maize" by Ellen Messer, pp. 97–112. Additional material adapted from "The History and Culture of Food and Drink in the Americas" by John C. Super and Louis Alberto Vargas, pp.1248–1254.

L. Patrick Coyle. *The World Encyclopedia of Food*. New York: Facts on File, 1982, p. 683.

O Paradise!: A Pastoral

Dante Alighieri. *The Divine Comedy*, *Paradiso*, Canto XXXI; *Inferno*, Canto II; *Paradiso*, Canto XXXIII. Translated by Henry Wadsworth Longfellow. In *The Works of Henry Wadsworth Longfellow*. Edited by Samuel Longfellow. New York: Houghton Mifflin, 1886–91.

Go, Go, Go

James Wright. "Autumn Begins in Martins Ferry, Ohio." In *Above the River: The Complete Poems*. 1990. New York and Lebanon, NH: Noonday and the University Press of New England, 1992.

Vince Lombardi. "Dinner Conversation with Vince Lombardi." In *The Vince Lombardi Scrapbook* by George L. Flynn. New York: Gosset and Dunlap, 1976, p. 23.

Official record of the capacity of Oklahoma Memorial Stadium during this period varies. I have decided to use 75,004 as the stadium capacity in this essay as it was the number most commonly cited. I ask that Sooner fans refrain from sending me any mail, unless flattery, regarding this matter.

Michael O'Brien. *Vince: A Personal Biography of Vince Lombardi*. New York: William Morrow, 1987, p. 205.

Peter Donahue. *The Cornelius Arms*. Seattle, WA: Missing Spoke, 2000.

Remember, She Said, the Magic

Walter Elias Disney. Quote from opening-day speech, July 17, 1955. Replicated on the Main Street USA Town Square flagpole dedication plaque. Official Disneyland Website, www.disneyland.com. An interesting fact worth noting is that, at the time of this writing, a Google.com search of "Disneyland" turned up some 1,050,000 hits. I am saddened to report that since the writing of this essay, a crash of the Big Thunder Mountain Railroad, caused by improper maintenance, claimed a life in 2003.